If Life Is
a Bowl of Cherries—
What Am I Doing
in the Pits?

Also Available in Large Print
by Erma Bombeck

*The Grass Is Always Greener
over the Septic Tank*

If Life Is a Bowl of Cherries— What Am I Doing in the Pits?

by
Erma Bombeck

G.K. HALL & CO.

Boston, Massachusetts

1978

Library of Congress Cataloging in Publication Data

Bombeck, Erma.
   If life is a bowl of cherries, what am I doing in the pits?

   "Published in large print."
   1.   Large type books.   I.   Title.
[PS3552.059I34   1978]   818'.5'407   78-15989
   ISBN 0-8161-6613-7

Published in Large Print by arrangement with McGraw-Hill Book Company.

Set in Photon 18 pt Crown

A number of the chapters in this book are based on material that has appeared elsewhere in another form.

*For my editor, Gladys Carr, who has
    the courage to laugh only when
    it's funny.*

*To my agent, Aaron Priest, who gives
    100 percent, but takes only
    10 percent.*

*For my Mom and Dad,
    (Albert and Erma Harris),
    who tell everyone their daughter
    is a successful dental assistant.*

Contents

Introduction

A Pair of White Socks
in a Pantyhose World

I've always worried a lot and frankly I'm good at it.

I worry about introducing people and going blank when I get to my mother. I worry about a shortage of ball bearings; a snake coming up through my kitchen drain. I worry about the world ending at midnight and getting stuck with three hours on a twenty-four-hour cold capsule.

I worry about getting into the Guinness World Book of Records under

1

"Pregnancy: Oldest Recorded Birth." I worry what the dog thinks when he sees me coming out of the shower, that one of my children will marry an Eskimo who will set me adrift on an iceberg when I can no longer feed myself. I worry about salesladies following me into the fitting room, oil slicks, and Carol Channing going bald. I worry about scientists discovering someday that lettuce has been fattening all along.

But mostly, I worry about surviving. Keeping up with the times in a world that changes daily. Knowing what to keep and what to discard. What to accept and what to protest.

Never, in the history of this country, have worriers had such a decade as the seventies. Each year has produced a bumper crop of worrierees larger than the year before and this year promises to be even better.

Children are becoming an endangered species, energy has reached crisis proportions, marriages are on the decline, and the only ones having any fun anymore are the research rats.

You cannot help but envy their decadence.

Throughout the years, these furry swingers have been plied with booze, pot, cigarettes, birth control pills, too much sun, cyclamates, caffeine, Red Dye No. 2, saccharine, disco music at ear-shock decibels, late nights, and a steady diet of snack food.

If people haven't asked themselves these questions, they should:

How come there are still more rats than people?

How come you've never seen an iron-starved, dull, listless rat drag around the house?

Did you ever see a rat with a salad in one hand and a calorie counter in the other; yet have you ever seen a fat rat?

Have you ever yelled at a rat who couldn't hear you and couldn't outrun you?

Did you ever see a rat drop dead with lipstick on his teeth?

These unanswered questions have bothered me because everytime I turn around a new research study is taking away something that has added to my pleasure in the past, but is bound to make me sick in the future.

I heard a story about a research rat recently that makes one pause and reflect. The rat's name was Lionel. He was a pro. He had everything tested on him from artificial sweeteners to bread preservatives to foot fungus viruses to brutal subway experiments and survived them all. A researcher figured he was something of a Superrat . . . an immortal who could sustain life no matter what the odds.

The researcher took him home as a pet for his children. Within three months, this indestructible rat was dead.

It seems that one day the rat was taken for a ride in the car with the teenage son who had a learner's permit. The rat died of a heart attack.

That's what this book is about. Surviving.

1

If You Thought the Wedding Was Bad . . .

Next to hot chicken soup, a tattoo of an anchor on your chest, and penicillin, I consider a honeymoon one of the most overrated events in the world.

It's one of those awkward times when you know everyone else had a better time than you did but you're too proud to admit it.

A Honeymoon Hall of Fame is being established at a resort hotel in the Poconos.

According to publicity, a heart-shaped alcove will feature photos, mementos and memorabilia of famed loving couples of history and fiction.

To date, they have included a recording of the Duke of Windsor's history-making declaration of love in which he renounced the British throne, early cartoons of Blondie and Dagwood, and film clips of Elizabeth Taylor's weddings.

It boggles the mind to imagine how they are going to determine who will enter the Honeymoon Hall of Fame and for what reasons, but here are a few nominations.

Ruth and Walter, who enjoyed the shortest honeymoon in history. Ruth shot Walter in the leg at the reception for fooling around with the maid of honor.

Sue and Ted for the most unique honeymoon in history. While Sue swam, danced, played tennis and shopped, Ted ice fished, skied, played cards and drank with the boys. While separate honeymoons don't work for everyone, it worked for Sue and Ted.

Laura and Stewart, the couple who were the greatest sports on their honeymoon. Right after the wedding, Laura discovered Stewart was out on bail for armed robbery, was coming down with three-day measles, was already married, had a son who set fires, and had taken out $75,000 worth of life insurance on her at the reception, but what the heck, as Laura explained, "Honeymoons are always a time of adjustment."

There are a lot of theories as to why marriages aren't lasting these days. The original premise was so simple. All you had to do was promise to love and to cherish from this day forward for better or for worse . . . and you asked yourself how bad could it get?

Bad never reaches it to the big stuff. It's always the little things that do a marriage in.

For example, a woman can walk through the Louvre Museum in Paris and see 5,000 breathtaking paintings on the wall. A man can walk through the Louvre Museum in Paris and see 5,000 nails in the wall. That is the inherent difference.

I don't know what there is about a nail in the wall that makes strong, virile men cry. The first time I was aware of this phenomenon was a week after my husband and I were married. I passed him in the kitchen one day while carrying a small nail and hammer.

"Where are you going with that hammer and nail?" he asked, beginning to pale.

"I am going to hang up a towel rack," I said.

He could not have looked more shocked if I had said I was going to drive a wooden peg into the heart of a vampire.

"Do you have to drive that spike into the wall to do it?"

"No," I said resting on the sink, "I could prop the towel rack up in a corner on the floor. I could hang it around my waist from a rope, or I could do away with it altogether and keep a furry dog around the sink to dry my hands on."

"What is there about women that they cannot stand to see a smooth, bare wall?" he grumbled.

"And what is there about men that they cannot stand to have the necessities of life hung from a wall?"

"What necessities?" he asked. "Certainly you don't need that mirror in the hallway."

"You said that about the light switches."

His eyes narrowed and I had the feeling he was going to zap me with his big point. "Do you realize," he asked slowly, "that there is not one single wall in this house where we can show a home movie?"

"Radio City Music Hall only has one," I retorted.

And so, the nail versus the bare wall has gone on for years at our house. He wouldn't hang a calendar over my desk because in twelve months the nail would become obsolete. He wouldn't hang the children's baby pictures because in two years they'd grow teeth and no one would recognize them. He wouldn't let me put a hook in the bathroom so I wouldn't have to hold my robe while I showered. He wouldn't let me hang a kitchen clock anywhere but on a wall stud (which happened to be located BEHIND the refrigerator).

Sometimes you have to wait for revenge. Yesterday, he reported he ran over a nail with his car.

There's an object lesson here, but I wouldn't insult anyone's intelligence by explaining it.

To love and to cherish from this day snoreward . . . foreward. Why doesn't anyone think to ask? Snoring could be a real threat to a marriage, especially if it's a snore that blows lampshades off the base, pictures off the wall, and makes farm animals restless as far as fifty miles away.

The loudest snore, according to the Guinness World Book of Records was measured at sixty-nine decibels at St. Mary's hospital in London.

Until last night.

That's when my husband broke the record by sustaining his breathing at a rousing seventy-two decibels. Seventy-two decibels, for the innocent, is the equivalent of having a cannon go off in the seat next to you in the Astrodome.

"Hey Cyrano," I yelled, "wake up. You're doing it again."

"Doing what?"

"Snoring."

"You woke me up to tell me that! If I've

10

told you once I've told you a thousand times, I do not snore. I'd know it if I did.''

''That is the same logic used by the man who said, 'If I had amnesia, I would have remembered it.' ''

''What did it sound like?''

''Like the Goodyear blimp with a slow leak.''

''Well, what did you expect? A concert?''

''Maybe I'll try what Lucille Farnsward tried when her husband's snoring drove her crazy.''

''What's that?'' he asked sleepily.

''She just put a pillow over his face.''

''Good Lord, woman, that would cause a man to stop breathing altogether.''

''Well, she hasn't worked the bugs out yet, but she's onto something.''

''Why don't you roll me over on my side?''

''I did and you hit me.''

And so it went, all through the night.

Frankly, I'm sick of all the therapist remedies that never seem to work, like self-hypnosis, earplugs and rolling the snorer off his back. These are the only remedies that bear consideration.

CHANGE BEDS

Get the snorer out of his own bed and into a strange one . . . preferably in another state.

PROLONGING SLEEP

This one works as well as any I've tried. Just as you are both climbing into bed, get every nerve in his body on alert by offhandedly mentioning, ''The IRS called you today, they'll call back tomorrow.''

Some experts believe you have to get to the root of a husband's reason for snoring. It has been suggested a person snores because he is troubled, his dentures don't fit properly, he indulges in excessive smoking or drinking, has swollen tonsils or suffers from old age.

Don't you believe any of it. A man snores for one reason alone . . . to annoy his wife. And if *that* doesn't do it, he'll resort to some other ploy to drive her crazy . . . the sorry-I'm-late syndrome.

There are no records to prove it, mind you, but I have every reason to believe my husband was an eleven-month baby.

And he's been running two months late ever since. Through marriage (and bad association) I have become a member of that great body of tardy Americans who grope their way down theater aisles in the dark, arrive at parties in time to drink their cocktails with their dessert, and celebrate Christmas on December 26.

Frankly, I don't know how a nice, punctual girl like me got stuck with a man who needs not a watch but a calendar and a keeper.

Would it shock anyone to know I have never seen a bride walk "down" the aisle? I have never seen a choir or a graduate in a processional? I have never seen the victim of a mystery BEFORE he was murdered. I have never seen a parking lot jammed with people. I have never seen the first race of a daily double, or a football team in clean uniforms.

The other night I had it out with my husband, "Look, I am in the prime time of my life and I have never heard the first thirty seconds of the "Minute Waltz." Doesn't that tell you something?"

"What are you trying to say?"

"I am trying to say that once before I die I would like to see a church with empty seats."

"We've been through all this before," he sighed. "Sitting around before an event begins is a complete waste of time when you could be spending it sleeping, reading and working."

"Don't forget driving around the block looking for a parking place. I don't understand you at all," I continued. "Don't you get curious as to what they put into first acts? Aren't you just a bit envious of people who don't have to jump onto moving trains? Aren't you tired of sitting down to a forty-four-minute egg each morning?"

"I set my alarm clock every night. What do you want from me?"

"I have seen you when you set your alarm clock. When you want to get up at six-thirty you set it for five-thirty. Then you reset it for six and when it goes off you hit it again and shout, 'Ha, ha, I was only kidding. I got another half-hour.' You reset it for six-thirty at which time you throw your body on it and say, 'I don't need you, I don't need anybody.' Then you go back to sleep."

"I just happen to believe there is no virtue in being early. What time is it?"

"It's eight o'clock. You're supposed to be at work at eight."

"Yes, lucky, I've got twenty minutes to spare."

Never in my life will I hear the "Star Spangled Banner" being played. I've also had to adjust to a man who does not know how to live in a world geared to leisure.

It's a common problem. A lot of women are married to workoholics and the trick is to get them to take two weeks off a year and just relax. Sounds simple?

I took my husband to the beach for two weeks where he promptly spread out a large beach towel, opened his briefcase and began to balance the checkbook.

I took him to a fancy hotel in a big city where he spent the entire week tinkering with the TV set trying to get the snow out of the picture.

Once I even took him to a nightclub where scantily clad girls danced out of key. After one came over and propped herself ceremoniously on his knee and tickled his chin, he turned to me and said, "We really should have the fire insurance on our house updated."

A friend of mine suggested I take him camping. "There is nothing like the wilderness to make a man relax and bring him back to nature." What did she know?

After three days in the wilderness, he had rotated the tires, mended three water mattresses, built a bridge, filled eight snow-control barrels with cinders and devised a sophisticated system to desand everyone before they entered the tent.

He went to the library to check on how the river got its name, wrote a letter to the editor of the local paper, read the lantern warranty out loud to all of us, organized a ball team and waxed the tent.

He alphabetized my staple goods, painted the word GAS on the gas cans, and hung our meat from a tree to make it inaccessible to bears and humans.

(Raccoons eventually ate it.)

After that experience, I told him, "Face it, Bunkie, we are incompatible."

"Why do you say that?" he asked.

"I'm a fun-loving, irrepressible, impetuous Zelda, and you are a proper, restrained, put-your-underwear-on-a-hanger Dr. Zhivago."

"I have a good time," he said soberly.

"Do you know I'm the only woman in the world to wake up on New Year's Day with nothing to regret from the night before? No gold wedgies scattered on the stairway, no party hats on the back of the commode, no taste in my mouth like a wet chenille tongue? Only the memories of Father Time dozing over a warm Gatorade. I have had more stimulating evenings picking out Tupperware."

"That not true," he said. "What did we do last New Year's Eve?"

"From seven to eight-thirty I picked bubble gum out of the dog's whiskers. At ten-thirty you fell asleep in the chair while I drank unflavored gelatin to strengthen my fingernails. At ten-forty-five I went to the refrigerator for a drink.

17

The kids had drunk all the mix and the neighbors had cleaned us out of the ice cubes. I poured two glasses of warm Gatorade, returned to the living room and kicked you in the foot. You jerked awake and said, 'Did you know that at midnight all horses age one year?'

"At eleven-forty-five your snooze alarm went off. You clicked your fingers while Carmen Lombardo sang 'Boo Hoo,' flipped the porch light on and off twice and shouted, 'Happy New Year.'

"I wish we could be like Dan and Wanda."

"What's so great about Dan and Wanda?" he asked.

"Wanda tells me she and Dan have meaningful conversations."

"Big deal," he yawned.

"It is a big deal. Have we ever had one?"

"I don't think so," he said.

Finally I said, "What *is* a meaningful conversation?"

"You're kidding! You actually don't know?"

"No, what is it?"

"Well, it's a conversation with meaning."

"Like an oil embargo or Paul Harvey?"

"Exactly."

"What about them?"

"What about who?"

"The oil embargo and Paul Harvey."

"It doesn't have to be a conversation about the oil embargo and Paul Harvey," he explained patiently. "It could be a discussion on anything in your daily schedule that is pertinent."

"I shaved my legs yesterday."

"That is not pertinent to anyone but you."

"Not really. I was using your razor."

"If you read the paper more, your conversation would be more stimulating."

"Okay, here's something meaningful. I read just yesterday that in Naples . . . that's in Italy . . . police were searching for a women who tried to cut off a man's nose with a pair of scissors while he was sleeping. What do you think of that?"

"That's not meaningful."

A few minutes later I said, "Suppose it was the American Embassy and the woman was a spy and the nose, which held secret documents about an oil embargo between Saudi Arabia and Paul Harvey, belonged to President Carter?"

"Why don't we just go back to meaningless drivel?" he said.

"Which reminds me," I said. "Did you read that article in the magazine where it said married people are unable to respond to their differences and that is why they become frustrated? It's called the old I-don't-care, it's-up-to-you or I-will-if-you-want-to-blues. You do that a lot, and I never know how you stand on things."

"I didn't read the article," he said.

"Well, as I recall, it suggested that a husband and wife spell out their feelings using a scale of one to ten. For example, if you say, 'Would you like to go to a movie?' instead of shrugging my shoulders and saying, 'Makes no difference,' I respond by saying, 'I'm five on attending a movie. Actually I'm eight on seeing the picture, but I'm three on spending the money right now.'"

"That makes sense."

"Let's try it. What would you like for dinner?"

"Farrah Fawcett Majors."

"Not 'who,' Clown, 'what'!"

"How will I know until I know what we're having?"

"That's the point. Offer some suggestions."

"Okay, liver is a big ten with me."

"I hate liver. To me liver is a minus two and you know it. How about meat loaf?"

"Meat loaf with meat is a six, without meat but with a lot of bread, a two. However, if you feel nineish about it, I'll send one of the kids to the Golden Arches, which is emerging as a big ten."

"Would it hurt you to be a nine about meat loaf just once?" I snapped.

"You should talk. In twenty-seven years, you haven't gotten off your two once when I have discussed having liver."

"Lower your voice! We don't have to air our two's and three's to the neighbors. How about an omelet?"

"That sounds like a firm eight to me."

"Good. We agree. We're out of eggs, so you'll have to go to the store."

"The car is a nine. I'm having battery trouble. That averages out omelets to a four."

"Okay, we're down to peanut butter. It's a definite three, minus one for being cold. However, it's a plus two for nutrition plus four for not being a leftover and a minus three for being fattening. That comes out to a five. Whatdaya think?"

"I don't care," said my husband.

"I was hoping you'd say that."

There's a lot of talk about why marriages are failing, but how come so many succeed?

Some women are too old for a paper route, too young for social security, too clumsy to steal and too tired for an affair. Some were just born into this world married and don't know how to act any different.

For the woman who has any doubts about her status, just answer a few simple questions.

When your husband's best friend leans

closer on the dance floor and whispers in your ear, "What are you doing the rest of my life?" and you whisper back, "Waiting for my washer repairman," you're married.

When a tall, dark, handsome stranger takes your hand and asks you to dance and you answer, "I can't. My pantyhose just shifted and with the slightest movement they'll bind my knees together," you're married.

When a Robert Redford look-alike invites you to have a cup of coffee after your evening class and you order a hamburger with onions, you're married.

When you are invited by the office single dude to join him for a weekend and bring a friend and you bring your husband . . . you're married.

When a party reveler asks, "Have you ever thought of leaving your husband" and you answer, "Where?" you're married.

No one talks about fidelity anymore, it's just something you hope is still around . . . and in significant numbers. And when the Coast Guard band strikes up "Semper

Fidelis'' and your husband says, ''They're
playing our song. You wanta dance?'' you
know you're married.

2

The Mother Mystique

An eleven-year-old girl once wrote:

Mrs. Bombeck,
I do not understand Mothers.
How come my Mom can hit anyone anywhere in the house at any distance with a shoe?
How can she tell without turning her head in the car that I am making faces at my brother in the back seat?
How can she be watching television in the living room and know that I am sneaking cookies in the kitchen?
Some of my friends also don't

understand Moms. They want to know how she can tell just by looking at them that they had a hot dog and three Cokes before they came home from school for dinner. Or where they are going to lose the sweater they hate.

We think it is spooky the way the phone rings and before we even pick it up she says, "Five minutes!"

We all agree no one in the world has super vision, super hearing, or can smell quite like a Mother. One guy said he had a piece of bubble gum once wrapped in foil in his shoe and his Mom said, "Let's have the gum. You want to tear your retainer out?"

Since you write about kids all the time we thought you could explain Moms to us.

Sincerely,
Cathie

Dear Cathie and Friends:

I found your letter most amusing. You make Motherhood sound like Jeane Dixon on a good day. (Sit up dear, and don't hold this book so close *to your face. You'll ruin your eyes.)*

Actually, there is no mystique at all to being a Mother. We all started out as normal, average little children like yourself, who grew up and developed the usual x-ray vision, two eyes in the back of our head, bionic hearing and olfactory senses that are sharpened by wet gym shoes. (Don't ask what "olfactory" is. Look it up in the dictionary.)

Mothers have never considered any of these senses a bonus. We call them instincts for survival. Without them we would be mortal and vulnerable. (Don't make such a face. It'll freeze that way and then where will you be?)

Someday, when your Motherhood genes develop, you too will know when someone is in the refrigerator even though you are at a PTA meeting. You will know shoes are wet and muddy when you can't even find them. You will sense your child is lying to you even while clutching a Bible in one hand, a rosary in the other and is standing under a picture of

Billy Graham.

Mothers are just normal people really. We don't pretend to be perfect or to have all the answers to childrearing.

Why, throughout the years, there are a lot of aspects of children for which I profess complete ignorance. For example . . .

Who Is I. Dunno?

Ever since I can remember, our home has harbored a fourth child — I. Dunno. Everyone sees him but me. All I know is, he's rotten.

"Who left the front door open?"

"I. Dunno."

"Who let the soap melt down the drain?"

"I. Dunno."

"Who ate the banana I was saving for the cake?"

"I. Dunno."

Frankly, I. Dunno is driving me nuts. He's lost two umbrellas, four pairs of boots and a bicycle. He has thirteen books overdue from the library, hasn't brought home a paper from school in three years, and once left a thermos of milk in the car for three weeks.

The other day the phone rang. I ran from the mailbox, cut my leg, tore off a fingernail in the door and got to the phone in time to see my son hanging up. "Who was it?" I asked breathlessly.

"I. Dunno. He hung up."

When I told my neighbor about it she said, "Cheer up. I've had an invisible child for years."

"What's his name?"

"Nobody."

"Is he rotten?"

"He makes Dennis the Menace look like a statue. He cracked the top of an heirloom candy dish, tears up the paper before anyone gets to read it, and once when I was driving the car pool, he nearly knocked me senseless with a ball bat."

"Ha!" I said bitterly, "you should have seen I. Dunno. He left thirteen lights burning the other night when he went out. *I* don't know how much longer I can stand it."

This morning at breakfast I said to my husband, "Who wants liver for dinner this evening?"

He looked up and said, "I dontcare."

That can only mean one thing. I. Dunno has a brother.

At What Age Is a Child Capable of Dressing Himself?

Some say when a child can reach the dirty clothes hamper without falling in, he is ready to assume responsibility for what he wears.

A child develops individuality long before he develops taste. I have seen my kid straggle into the kitchen in the morning with outfits that need only one accessory: an empty gin bottle.

There is always one child in the family who thrives on insecurities and must have her emotional temperature taken every five minutes. I call it the "Parade of the Closet." Beginning at 7 A.M. she will appear at breakfast fully clothed and ready for school. Before the cereal has stopped exploding in the bowl, she has disappeared to her room and is in another complete outfit. Four words from her mother ("You look nice today") and she is off again to her bedroom in tears for still another complete change.

She plays the same musical clothes until she runs out of clothes/the bus leaves/her mother is institutionalized . . . whichever comes first.

There is always the kid who has an aversion to clean clothes. He is allergic to creases in trousers, socks that have soft toes, underwear that is folded, and sweaters you can sniff without passing out. He's the child who always applauds the Ring Around the Collar commercials.

The opposite is the youngster who neither desires what is in his closet nor what is in the dirty clothes hamper. He wants what has to be ironed. I have always said, "If I had nothing in my ironing bag but a diaper, that kid would wear a top hat and go to school dressed as the New Year."

Last year, we allowed our children to

pack their own suitcases for our vacation. One wore a baseball cap and a pair of brown corduroys for an entire week. (We told everyone he had brain surgery.)

Another brought one coat . . . an old army jacket belonging to his father. (He looked like a deserter from the other side.) The other one packed one pair of shoes . . . a red-white-and-blue pair of sneakers with stars. The only time he didn't look out of place was under a basket in a coliseum.

Last week, all three of my children looked worse than usual as they headed for the door. "Why do all of you look so rotten today?" I asked. "Are you in a school play or something?"

"No, we're having our class pictures taken."

It figures.

Haven't I Always Loved Whatshisname Best?

A woman starts thinking of a name for

her baby from the minute she knows she is carrying one. She will write it out, say it aloud, try it out on her friends, and embroider it on little shirts. When the baby is born she will whisper the name softly in its ear, write it on dozens of announcements and file it in the courthouse records.

A few years and a few kids later, she can't remember who you are.

I've heard mothers go through ten or twelve names before they get lucky and hit the right one. (Once I wore my P.J.s wrong side out and my mom, thinking it was a name tag, called me Dr. Denton for a week.)

Children seem to think there is something Freudian in the entire exercise. The old if-my-mother-really-loved-me-she'd-remember-my-name trauma. This is hogwash. I love Marc . . . Mary . . . Mike . . . Mil . . . Massa . . . whatshisname with the same affection as I love Bet . . . Bronc . . . Evely . . . Mar . . . Tri . . . you know who you are.

Our neighborhood psychiatrist bears me out. He said there is nothing you can generalize from mothers who can't put a name to their children right off the bat.

It used to be a good day for me when I could remember what I called them for, let alone remember who they are.

In talking with a young married the other day, it was revealed that he was one of seven children and not once when he was growing up was he ever called by his real name. "I guess it was because there were so many of us," he said, "that it confused my mother."

I hated to shoot his theory down, but for a long while I was an only child and still got Sara . . . Bet . . . Mild . . . Vir . . . Edna. Finally, in desperation, my mother would shout, "How long do I have to call you before you answer?"

I'd yell back, "Until you get it right."

"Was I close?" she'd shout.

"Edna was somewhere in the neighborhood."

"I always liked Edna," she mused. "I should have named you that."

"Then why did you name me Erma?"

"Because it was easy to remember."

"Why Can't We Have Our Own Apartment?"

We knew the kids would take it the wrong way, but we had to do it anyway.

"Children," we said, "your father and I want to get our own apartment."

One looked up from his homework and the other two even turned down the volume on the TV set. "What are you saying?"

"We are saying we'd like to move out and be on our own for a while."

"But why?" asked our daughter. "Aren't you happy here? You have your own room and the run of the house."

"I know, but a lot of parents our age are striking out on their own."

"It'll be expensive," said our son. "Have you thought about utilities and phone bills and newspapers and a hundred little things you take for granted around here?"

"We've thought it all through."

"Spit it out," said our daughter. "What's bothering you about living with us? Did we ask too much? What did we ask you to do? Only cook, make beds, do laundry, take care of the yard, keep the cars in running order and bring in the money. Was that so hard?"

"It's not that," I said gently. "It's just that we want to fix up our own apartment and come and go as we please."

"If it's your car you wanted, why didn't you say so? We could make arrangements."

"It's not just the car. We want to be able to play our stereos when we want to and come in late without someone saying, 'Where have you been?' and invite people over without other people hanging around eating our chip dip."

"What will you do for furniture?"

"We don't need all that much. We'll just take a few small appliances, some linens, our bedroom suite, the typewriter, the luggage, the card table and chairs, the old TV you never use, and some pots and pans and a few tables and chairs."

"You'll call everyday?"

We nodded.

As we headed for the car I heard one

son whisper sadly, "Wait till they get their first utility bill. They'll be back."

Is There a Life After Mine?

No one knows what her life expectancy is, but I have a horror of leaving this world and not having anyone in the entire family know how to replace a toilet tissue spindle.

It's an awesome thought to have four grown people wandering around in a daze saying, "I thought she told you how," and another saying, "If I knew she was sick, I'd have paid attention."

The tissue spindle isn't the only home skill that has been mastered by no one at our house. Consequently, I have put together a single family survival manual when Mom is gone.

REPLACING TOILET TISSUE SPINDLE

Grasp old spindle and push gently to one side where there is a spring action. The spindle will release and you discard the old cardboard. Slip on new roll and insert one end of spindle in the spring-action side and listen for a click into place.

WASHING TOOTHPASTE
OFF SIDE OF WASHBOWL

Before toothpaste is allowed to harden/become a permanent part of the enamel, swish water from faucet over affected areas and give a gentle nudge with washcloth or hands. Sink will be ready for next slobee.

TURNING ON THE STOVE

Hot meals require a hot stove. If the stove is gas, ignite by turning dial or handle while holding match over burner. If stove is electric, take forefinger and push firmly on button of desired heat. Caution: Do not put food directly on burner, but put it in a pan first.

CLOSING A DOOR

This looks harder than it is. When door is ajar, make sure it is free of foreign objects (children, feet, packages), then grasp it firmly by the handle and give it a push until you hear it click. Slamming the door will not make it close any firmer than a push.

TURNING OFF A LIGHT

The same principle is used in turning off a light as in turning it on. If it is a wall switch, you flick the switch up or down until you no longer see the light. If it is a chain mechanism, you compress chain between thumb and forefinger and give it a tug. The light will extinguish.

OPERATING A CLOTHES HAMPER

Don't be intimidated because there are no dials or instructions on the lid. Bending from the waist you simply pick up a sock, a pair of pants, or a towel, lift the lid of the hamper and feed soiled clothes into it.

The Good Fairy will take it from there.

Keep this manual handy for easy references. If I have to take these skills with me when I go . . . I'm not going.

"Why Can't Our Average Little Family Get Their Own TV Series?"

The other night I was watching a situation comedy series of a typical, American family. This family laughed until they got sick.

Everytime Daddy opened his mouth, he was a scream. The mother was a stitch. And the kids were absolute geniuses at spewing out hilarious retorts. I looked around at our group. My husband was deeply depressed over the paper. He's looked like that since he let his G.I. insurance lapse. One child was on the phone insisting, "I don't believe it!" every minute and a half. Another was locked in his room with the stereo on and the other was staring morosely into the refrigerator waiting for something to embrace him.

"You know the trouble with this family? We're not funny. All the other families in the world are sitting around throwing away one-liners and having a barrel of laughs. The six o'clock news gets more laughs than we do. We've got to get with it or we'll never get our own series."

The next night as I heard my husband's car in the driveway, I shouted, "Hey Gang. Heeeeeeereeeeee's Daddy!"

"Well," said our son, "if it isn't our father whose wallet is full of big bills . . . all unpaid."

"What's the matter with you?" asked my husband. "You're on your feet. Has your car been repossessed?"

"Dyyyyyynnnnnoooomite!" said our youngest. (I almost fell out of the chair.)

"Hey, Mom," said a son, "what do you get if you take a fender from a Chevy, the chrome from a Ford and the hubcaps from a Pontiac?" I shook my head.

"Six months!"

"A rubber hose up your nose," I said amid laughter.

"So," said my husband, "I thought you

were going to straighten up the house."

"Why?" I said nudging him in his ribs. "Is it tilted? Incidentally, did you hear Mel just got a poodle for his wife?"

"I wish I could make a trade like that."

"Hey, Dad," said our daughter, "the dog just ate Mom's meatloaf."

"Don't cry," he said, "I'll buy you another dog."

My mother poked her head in the door. "Got any coffee?"

We all slumped in our chairs exhausted. Thank God for commercials.

3

Who Killed
Apple Pie?

It's a frightening feeling to wake up one morning and discover that while you were asleep you went out of style.

That's what happened to millions of housewives, who one day looked into their mirrors and said, "I do not feel fulfilled putting toilet seats down all day."

Women were sick of pushing buttons. Besides, the buttons were pushing back. There was a housewife in Michigan who was vacuuming her carpet one morning and leaned over to pick an object off the floor. Her hair was pulled into the machine by the underside brush roller, causing her to fall on top of the vacuum and sustain electrical shock to the left side of her head.

They no longer bought the theory, advanced by a British Medical Association, that doing housework was the secret to female longevity and that all that exercise would prolong life.

As I was on my knees one afternoon, hoisting the bunk beds on my back and trying to put the slats back into the grooves, my husband asked, "What are you doing down there?"

"Prolonging my life," I said dryly.

"Those things fall out all the time," he said. "Why don't you get some slats that are longer?"

"They were longer when we got them," I said.

"Are you going to start that business about inanimate things being human? You're going bananas being cooped up in this house. You should get out more. After you get all this stuff fixed up around here, why don't you do something you've always wanted to do?"

I sat back on my knees and reflected.

What I always wanted to do was run away from home. You all know the feeling. You diet for two weeks and gain three pounds. You break your bottom to get to a White Sale only to discover that all they have left are double top sheets, single contour bottoms, and King pillowcases.

Your best friend (whom you have always trusted) calls and tells you she just found out how to bake bread. Some wise guy just wrote "HELP" in the dust on the draperies.

You pick up a movie magazine in the supermarket with headlines reading JACKIE ONASSIS' SPENDING HABITS SUGGEST MENTAL DISORDER and realize you've had the same disorder for years.

The cheerleader on your high school cheer squad just became a grandmother. The supermarket just discontinued your silverware pattern and you spend forty minutes ironing a linen dress and it doesn't fit you anymore.

You drive into a drive-in bank and the car just ahead of you gets a flat. You see your neighbor going to the office and yell,

"I hope you find eraser droppings in your IBM Selectric." And you can't take it anymore.

Then one day in a leading magazine, I saw a story called, "Today's Woman on the Go."

At the top of the article was a picture of a well-stacked blonde at a construction site with a group of men around her while she read blueprints to them. I noted her shoes were coordinated with her Gucci yellow hard hat.

The second picture showed her in a pair of flowing pajamas standing over the stove stirring her filet-mignon helper (recipe on page 36) while her husband tossed the salad and her children lovingly set the table.

It made me want to spit up.

I wanted to be "on the go." (I was half-gone already.) Imagine! Every morning going off to carpetland . . . to fresh bread for lunch . . . to a phone that wasn't sticky with grape jelly . . . to perfume behind each knee that spelled madness to stock boys.

And I said to myself, "There, but for the

grace of a babysitter go I."

Once I made up my mind, I interviewed sitters for six months. It's depressing when you realize no one wants to be paid for what you've been doing for years for nothing. I talked with one who could only work until the children came home from school. Another believed in naps until age thirty-five, and there was one who worked for one day and quit saying, "Do you actually expect me to work in a house where the water jug looks like snow falling in a paperweight?"

Other women, I was to discover, had the same problem. A friend of mine who is a registered nurse said she had a shattering experience. She found a "gem" who was willing to sit with her children if she left explicit instructions. The first day she left the following note:

"Greg gets 1 tsp. of pink medicine in refrigerator at 8 A.M. and before lunch. He has impetigo, so wash your hands good with soap and water and don't let him use anyone else's glass.

"Paula gets 1 tsp. of orange medicine

in brown bottle at 8 A.M. and at lunch. There's plenty of lunch meat, peanut butter, etc., for lunch.

"Paula has to be taken to the potty every two to three hours. There's a potty seat upstairs and a small chair in Rec. Room.

"Don't let dog in the chewing gum. He craves it but has to be taken to the vet to remove. He gets pills once a day (not birth control) for slight infection. Get Frank (who is in and out all day long) to hold him so he will not bite.

"Take messages. Don't use toilet in utility room. It bubbles. If you have questions, call me. Tell them you are one of the nurses if they ask."

When she arrived home, the door was marked with lamb's blood and there was a large quarantine sign tacked on it. The sitter had fled.

You have only to work once in your life to know that "Today's Woman on the Go" is pure fiction. Maybe they got the captions under the pictures switched.

Maybe she wore the long flowing pajamas at work and the hard hat at home. Heaven knows, home is a Hard Hat area.

Where were the pictures showing her racing around the kitchen in a pair of bedroom slippers, trying to quick-thaw a chop under each armpit and yelling like a shrew, "All right, you guys, I know you're in the house. I can hear your stomachs growling."

According to the article, all you needed was a worksheet, with everyone in the family having his or her own responsibility, leaving Mother time not only to hold down a full-time job, but to paint, sew her own coats, ride horses, and run for the U.S. Senate.

It wasn't like that at all. I called home one evening and said, "Let me speak to your father."

"He's at the dentist," said my son. "He chipped his tooth this morning on the frozen bread."

"So who was on the worksheet to defrost the bread?"

"I was, but I forgot my key, got locked out and stayed all night with Mike. The milkman got locked out too. There are twelve half-gallons of milk in the garage.''

''Where's your sister?''

''I made her bed with her in it. She's not speaking. There are wet clothes in the washer and they're covered with a brown rash. We're defrosting the spareribs under your hairdryer. Guess who forgot to put the dog out when he came home? When are you coming home?''

''I'll be home tomorrow. Do you miss me?''

''No, but according to the worksheet, you're on for dishes.''

Sharing responsibility is what the entire movement to free women is all about. If women are ever to be appreciated, a husband should drive a car pool . . . just once.

Transporting children is my husband's twenty-sixth favorite thing. It comes somewhere between eating lunch in a tea room and dropping a bowling ball on his foot.

''Remember,'' I warned him before his first attempt, ''they are small children

. . . not mail sacks. That means you have to bring the car to a complete stop and open the door for them. Don't shout and be sure to give all six of them their own window. Good luck.''

An hour-and-a-half later as he staggered through the door I said,

"So, what took you so long?"

"To begin with, old paste breath didn't want to get into the car. He said his mother didn't want him to ride with strangers. Then the name tag that was pinned to whatshername's dress fell off and she didn't know who she was. Debbie cried for three blocks because she left her Bionic Woman lunchbox on the swings. Cecil . . . I guess that's his name . . . the one who sits there and rebuttons his sweater all the time trying to make it come out even . . ."

"That's Cecil."

"He told me he lived at the Dairy Queen."

"So what took you so long?"

"Michael. Michael is the one who took me so long. He said he didn't know

where he lived, so to make friends, I gave him a taffy sucker. I must have driven around in circles for thirty minutes before he said, 'That's my house.'

"Michael," I said, "we've passed this house twenty to thirty times. Why didn't you say something before?"

"Because," he said, "I'm not allowed to talk with food in my mouth."

There are some who say giving children responsibility makes them grow. There are others who contend it increases your insurance rates.

Whatever, there are some ground rules that must prevail while a mother is employed outside the home. First, when to bug and when not to bug. In other words, when do you call Mom on the phone at work?

Emergencies do arise. There's no doubt about that, but some guidelines must be established at the top of the page.

Before a child calls his mother at work he must ask himself: (1) Will Mom drop dead when she hears this? (2) Can she find a plumber after five? (3) Will she carry out her threat to move to another city and change her name?

If the answers are "Yes, No, Yes," the child might try putting the incident in a proper perspective.

For example, if there is blood to report, consider these questions, Is it his? His brother's? Is there a lot? A little? On the sofa that is not Scotchgarded? Or the eighty-dollar one that they are still making payments on? Will the bleeding stop? Was it an accident? A loose baby tooth? Can he shut up about it and pass it off as an insect bite?

Another example: When every other kid in the neighborhood decides your child's house would be a neat place to play because there is no adult at home, he should ask himself, "Do I want to spend my entire puberty locked in my room with no food and no television? Do I need the friendship of a boy who throws ice cubes at the bird? Will Mom notice we made confetti in her blender?

Other situations to be definite about:

When a group of children decide to wash

the cat and put him in the dryer and want to know what setting to use . . . CALL.

When he and his brother are hitting and slapping over the last soft drink and he wants a high level decision on who gets it. DON'T CALL.

When a couple of men in a pickup truck tell him his Mom is having the TV slipcovered, the silverware stored, her jewelry cleaned and his ten-speed bicycle oiled, CALL . . . AND FAST.

When his sister chases him into the house with the garden hose and the furniture is turning a funny looking white, RUN.

When he is bored and has nothing to do and just wants to talk, CALL HIS FATHER.

During the summer months when children are too old for a sitter and too young for sense, I find that a Primer for Imaginative Children is a must just to set down what you expect of them.

Primer for Imaginative Children

This is a house.

Vehicles are not permitted in the house.

Occupancy of this house by more than two hundred people is dangerous and unlawful. Violators will be prosecuted.

There is a dog in the house. His name is Spot. Spot likes to run and play and chase sticks. He also likes to relieve himself with some regularity. Watch Spot for telltale signs of urgency, such as jumping higher than the ceiling, gnawing on the doorknob or tunneling under the door.

It is fun to eat. See the milk? See the butter? See the lunch meat? They cannot run. They cannot walk. They have no legs. They must be picked up and returned to the refrigerator or they will turn green. Green is not a happy color.

Hear the phone ring? That means someone wants to talk to you. Ring. Ring. Ring. When the phone rings, pick it up and speak directly into it. Say "Hello." Say "Goodbye." Say anything.

A bedroom is a special place. Find your bed each day. Try. Sometimes, you cannot see your bed because it is covered with clutter. This is not healthy. A cluttered room is a messy room. Fish die in a messy room. Mothers cannot breathe in a messy room. A messy room is unfit for humans. Many people in this house are human.

A bathroom is your friend. It is there when you need it. Lids do not like to be standing all the time. They get tired. Towels do not like to be on the floor. They cannot see anything. Ugh. Soap does not like to lie in a drain and melt. Boo.

See Mommy come home. See Daddy come home. They are walking on their knees. Be kind to Mommy and Daddy. ''Look, look, Mommy, Bruce is bloody. I'm telling, Debbie. I didn't do it, Daddy.''

Do you want to make Mommy crazy?

Do you want to make Daddy rupture a neck vein?

Then shape up, up, up.

The controversy of whether to work outside the home or not to work outside the home goes on. Each woman in her own way assesses what her needs are, and how they can best be met.

It must be pointed out that office procedure also has its shortcomings. Nothing is perfect. For example, one office had the following SICK LEAVE POLICY.

SICKNESS

No excuse. We will no longer accept your doctor's statement as proof, as we believe if you are able to go to the doctor, you are able to come to work.

DEATH (other than your own)

This is no excuse. There is nothing you can do for them and we are sure that someone else in a lesser position can attend to arrangements. However, if the funeral can be arranged in the late afternoon, we will be glad to let you off one hour early, provided your share of work is ahead enough to keep the job going in your absence.

DEATH (your own)

This is acceptable as an excuse provided (a) two weeks' notice is given in order to break in a new person for your job (b) if two weeks' notice is not possible, call in before 8 A.M. so that a sub may be provided and (c) this must be verified by your doctor's signature and your own. Both signatures must be present, or the time will be deducted from your annual sick leave.

LEAVE OF ABSENCE (for an operation)

We are no longer allowing this practice. We wish to discourage any thought you may have about needing an operation. We believe that as long as you are employed here, you will need all of whatever you have and should not consider having anything removed. We hired you as you are, and to have anything removed would certainly make you less than we bargained for.

LEAVE OF ABSENCE (rest room)

Too much time is being spent in the rest rooms. Our time study man has ascertained that three minutes, fifteen seconds constitutes a generous break. In the future, we will follow the practice of going to the rest room in alphabetical order. Those with names beginning with A will go from 8 A.M. to 8:05, 15 seconds; those with F from 8:03, 15 seconds to 8:06, 30 seconds, etc. If you miss your turn, you must wait until the day when your turn comes again.

As I was on my knees one afternoon at the office, trying to lift a filing cabinet over a piece of carpet, my boss asked, "What are you doing down there?"

"Prolonging my life. I just read a survey where it said women who worked outside the home lived a richer, fuller, longer life."

"You look tired to me," he said. "Why don't you get out of the office for a while. Go home, bake a little bread, wax the floors, visit with your children."

Between keeping house and working, I'm probably going to live to be a hundred. Or maybe it will just seem that long.

4

The Varicose Open

Well, if I had known the battle of the sexes was going to be fought on a tennis court, I wouldn't have let my knees grow together.

Looking back, it all started when Bobby Riggs became Queen of the Courts (grass, clay, and Margaret). Businessmen, housewives, students, blue-collar workers, politicians, preschoolers, everyone was "into tennis."

Heaven help you if you were new to the game. It was an uphill battle to break through the barriers of snobbery and elitism to play a game that for years had been dominated by rich kids with weak chins and straight, white teeth.

That sounds biased, but did you ever see a picture of Rockefeller coming out of a bowling alley with his gym bag, or a Kennedy tinkering with his engine just before his stock car race? On the coldest day in the midwest you could always pick up a newspaper and see one of them with a white sweater knotted around his neck, shading his eyes from the blazing sun.

As a nuevo tennis player, I felt like Belle Watling (the madam in Gone with the Wind who tried to buy respectability by giving money to a hospital). The question was could a woman plagued by varicose veins find happiness with a tennis player who was attached to his mother by an umbilical sweatband?

My first day out was a disaster. I encountered a member of the First Family of tennis who appraised me coolly.

"White is tacky," she sniffed. "Everyone but everyone who plays tennis these days dresses in colors. Tell me, who is your pro?"

"I've been getting a little help with my strokes from Leroy Ace."

She frowned, "I don't believe I've heard of him. What club?"

"The boy's club. But he moonlights from his garage."

"How well do you play?" she asked before going to the other side of the net.

"I had tennis elbow twice last week."

"That only means something is wrong with your stroke. You need help. Do you prefer string or gut?"

"I'll play with anybody," I shrugged.

"Would you like to warm up?"

"Sure," I popped a ball over the fence. "Would you believe I've only been playing for two days?"

"That long?" she said tiredly.

"What about you?" I asked.

"I played in the good old days," she said slowly, "before they opened up the courts to Democrats."

I didn't care what she said. I knew that, somehow, in this lumpy little body that tripped over lint in the carpet was a Chrissie Evert just fighting to get out.

It was just a matter of time before I

developed a form, learned how to get my racket out of the press, and didn't require oxygen after each serve.

But first, I knew I would never be taken seriously as a tennis player until I learned how to pick up the ball. I summoned my son.

Now, there are few things in this world more satisfying than having your son teach you how to play tennis. One is having a semitruck run over your foot.

It's almost as if he is paying you back for letting him fall off the dryer when he was a baby . . . for putting him to bed on his fifth birthday when he threw ice cream into the fan . . . for bailing out of the car when you were teaching him how to drive. All the hostilities come out the moment you walk onto the court together.

"Okay, we're going to continue today with our instruction on how to pick up the ball."

"I know how to pick up the ball," I said.

"I've told you before, we do not pick up the ball like a gorilla going for a banana. There is a professional way and there are several approaches. You can learn with the western forehand grip. Lean over gently and tap the ball with your racket until it bounces."

Several minutes later as I was on my knees pounding the racket into the yellow optic, he leaned over and said, "It's not a snake you are beating to death. It is a tennis ball. Let's try the ball-against-the-foot method."

I stood up exhausted. "How does that work again?"

"You grip your racket against the ball and firmly force it to the inside of your left foot. Bending your knee, you lift the ball to about six inches off the ground and drop it. When it bounces, you continue bouncing it with your racket until you can pluck it off the ground and into your hand."

Gripping the racket, I forced the ball to the inside of my foot where it rolled over the foot and toward the net. I cornered it and started inching the ball up my leg, but lost my balance and fell into the net.

Approaching the ball once more I accidentally kicked it with my foot and, in a crouched position, I chased it to the corner of the court, slamming my body into the fence.

For the next fifteen minutes, the elusive little ball moved all over the court like it had a motor in it.

Finally, I leaned over, grabbed it with my hand, placed it on my leg and supported it with the racket.

"Okay," I shouted, "I picked up the ball."

"That'll be all for today," he said. "We'll spend a few more weeks on this before moving along to hitting the ball."

I put my arm over his shoulder, "Now, let me tell you how to pick the towels off the bathroom floor. You simply bend your body in the middle, grasp the towel firmly between . . ."

He was gone.

Rotten kids. They shouldn't be allowed on the courts. I got a theory about these kids who play tennis anyway . . . You know the ones. These little tiny kids who sit around swanky tennis courts in a pair of dollar-ninety-eight tennis shoes with the strings knotted, holding a tennis racket, made in Tijuana and sucking on an ice cube. When they are invited to play, they squint and ask, "What do you call this thing again?"

The adults are amused. "A tennis racket."

Then the kid really starts to perform. He giggles as his pudgy little hands cannot hold two tennis balls at the same time, so he places one on the base line. He has to be told where to stand and his form is somewhere between Art Buchwald and a bullfighter with bad eyes.

After the warm-up, the personality of the kid changes. He scoops up the ball with the back of his foot, aces his opponent on every serve, runs around the court like a wood nymph, jumps the net to offer his condolences and asks for a towel.

My theory is they're beings from another planet who aren't children at all. They're forty-nine-year-old tennis players who have the body of a six-million-dollar man.

They get on my nerves almost as much as Debbie Dominant. Debbie has always been a pace setter. She was the first woman on the block with wheels on her garbage cans and chewed on her sunglasses three years before Marlo Thomas.

Two years before tennis became "in," Debbie appeared at the supermarket flushed and breathless in a tennis dress up to her tan line and white tennis shoes with a little ball fringe over the heel.

"Isn't this terrible?" she said, pushing her white hat back on her head. "I was at set point and before I knew it the dinner hour was upon me and I just buzzed in here before I could change. I had no idea I'd meet anyone I knew. I'm simply MORTIFIED!"

If she was Lady Godiva riding a power mower she couldn't have been less obvious.

Within weeks, every housewife in the neighborhood was in tennis dress not only while pushing her shopping cart around, but wearing it everywhere.

At school one afternoon, I passed a housewife in the hall who was headed for the office in full tennis attire. "Excuse me," I said, "But the girl's rest room is out of paper towels."

"Why tell me?" she asked, nervously fingering her sweatband.

"You had 'HEAD' on your T-shirt, and I figured you were a rest-room attendant."

"You're obviously not into tennis," she said stiffly.

That was the day I succumbed. I have been "into" tennis now for six months and was named Miss Congeniality in the Varicose Open.

Although my form still needs work (the body, not the game), I am proud to report I have made progress.

To begin with, I have finally mastered what to do with the second tennis ball. Having small hands, I was becoming terribly self-conscious about keeping it in a can in the car while I served the first one. I noted some women tucked the second ball just inside the elastic leg of their tennis panties. I tried, but found the space already occupied by a leg. Now, I simply drop the second ball down my cleavage, giving me a chest that often stuns my opponent throughout an entire set.

Next, I have learned how to stall, thus

throwing my opponent's entire game off. It's called the old tie-the-shoe trick. When your opponent is ready to serve, simply drop to your knees, untie your shoe, rearrange its tongue and tie it again. Baseball players use the old stall all the time. (Recently, Pat Zachry swallowed his chewing tobacco and threw up against a dugout wall. I haven't mastered at what hour I can throw up yet. Sometimes it is during a return.)

Another play is the rearrange-the-string number. Never take the rap for a bad return or no return. Whenever you hit a ball into the net, or miss it entirely, bring the game to a grinding halt by checking the strings of your racket, spending sometimes as much as five minutes separating them and testing their strength. This absolves you of any of the responsibility for a bad shot.

Forget all you have been told about concentration. It's overrated. Often, when there is time during one of my lobs, I yell across the net, "Your zipper is open," and have not only been ignored, but soundly punished, for my good deed.

Probably the greatest accomplishment this year has been my skill at learning how to run around my backhand. Early in my tennis career, I used to think when a ball landed to the left of me I had to use my backhand to return it. I have since learned that anything is better, including straddling a fifteen-foot cyclone fence.

No doubt about it . . . every day in every way, my game grows stronger. I saw one enthusiast the other day playing with his racket out of the press. I'll have to try that.

5

Profile of a Martyress

When the martyresses of our time are being immortalized, there's no doubt a shrine will be erected to the mother who holds down the homefront while her husband travels.

This courageous woman who singlehandedly battles magazine salesmen, juggles car pools, stands up to TV repairmen, and whose deft fingers can find a fuse box in the darkness.

As with most heroines, there are few who are appreciated in their lifetime. One cannot possibly understand the awesome responsibility they shoulder.

That is why I should like to nominate overworked, underpatienced, unappreciated Lorraine Suggs . . . Mother Martyress.

If any of us walked for a week in her wedgies, we might have the following story to tell:

Monday she went to a parent-teacher conference alone to be told her son stole paper towels from the rest room (the girls'), wrote an obscene word in the dust on Mr. Gripper's car, and was flunking lunch. She said her husband traveled a lot and the teacher said:

"You should be glad he's working."

On Tuesday, the dog got hit by a motorcycle, the house payment got lost in the mail and her daughter tried to crush a tin can with her hand like the Bionic Woman and required a tetanus shot. She told the doctor her husband traveled a lot and he said:

"You're lucky you have a car."

On Wednesday, the television set blew a tube, the car developed a wheeze and she had to cancel a night out with the girls. Her mother-in-law said:

"Be thankful you have children."

On Thursday, she was making a left-hand turn in her VW Rabbit, when a car plowed into the back of her. As she sat there crying softly, "The rabbit died . . . the rabbit died . . ." a police officer stuck his head in the window and said:

"You're lucky lady. No one got hurt."

On Friday at the supermarket, so bored she was carrying on a conversation with a broom display, she went through the mechanics of shopping . . . lashing one kid to the basket, getting another out of the bean display where he "found" a hole in a bag of pinto beans, and on finding the third had eaten an unknown amount of fruit, offered to weigh him and anything over fifty-three pounds, pay the difference. The checkout girl in noting all the convenience foods said:

"You're lucky to have your husband gone a lot. At least you don't have to cook big meals."

On Saturday, she car pooled it to the Little Leagues, two haircuts, one dental appointment, baton-twirling lessons, the cleaners, the post office and a birthday party. As she started the power mower at dusk, a neighbor yelled over the fence:

"You're lucky. At least you get out of the house."

On Sunday, she dragged the brood to church. The baby chewed up two verses out of the hymnal, one child followed a rolling dime all the way to the altar, and the third stole a sponge from the Holy Water font.

The minister stood at the door, smiled stiffly and said:

"You should be thankful the good Lord is looking after you."

Profile of a Martyr

When the martyrs of our time are being immortalized, there's no doubt a shrine will be erected to the man who must leave the comforts of his home and travel.

This courageous soul, who sits around airports waiting for a glimpse of O.J. Simpson, and misses his plane because a security buzzer keeps picking up the foil on his gum wrapper.

This saint of a man, who spends hours in

hotels trying to locate the switch that will give him light, who adjusts the shower so that it directs the spray INSIDE the tub.

As with most heroes, there are few who are appreciated in their lifetime. One cannot possibly understand the frustrations they shoulder.

That is why I should like to nominate overworked, underpaid, unappreciated Tom Suggs . . . Father and Martyr who makes his living attending conventions.

If any of us walked for a week in his shoes, we might have the following story to tell:

Monday: He checked into the hotel, which has no washcloths, a refrigerator in the bathroom growing penicillin . . . a balcony that faces a brick wall, a TV set that gets extension courses in math from the university and an air-conditioner—heater with a broken thermometer. There are no light switches. When he summoned the maid she said:

"You should be glad you're not next to the hospitality suite."

Tuesday: The hotel is a floating ark

with two of everything, including elevators. There are five hundred and twenty-five rooms and fifteen hundred conventioneers. The meetings are scheduled in the Promenade room, which is on the mezzanine between the third and fourth floors and is serviced by elevator no. 1 between the hours of 3 and 4 A.M. No one knows this. He complained to another conventioneer, who said:

"You're lucky. I made it to yesterday's meeting."

Wednesday: After two days of conversing with chests that say, "Hello there, my name is illegible," he tries to call home only to find the hotel operator is unlisted. He walks to the desk, places the call and waits fifteen minutes while his pre-schooler goes to "get mommy," five more minutes while she coaxes the baby to say, "Hi Daddy," and another twenty minutes listening to a report on how his house died due to his negligence.

The operator observes:

"You're lucky she puts up with you."

Thursday: His luggage still hasn't arrived, but there is a tracer who suspects it has never left the airport at home. As he sits in his room, trying to heat up a "rare" hamburger on a TV set that is flashing math equations, the phone rings and it is a sloshed buddy from the hospitality suite shouting:

"Hey, buddy, this beats cutting grass, doesn't it?"

Friday: He sits through five keynote speeches, comparable only to waking up in a recovery room and being asked to applaud. He still cannot find the light switch. The maid says:

"You're lucky. A man's wife down the hall arrived unexpectedly and found his light switch at 2 this morning. She nearly killed him."

Saturday he took two taxis full of clients to dinner at which a record was set for carrying on conversation without saying one thing that was worth repeating. He called his wife again, who said:

"Thank God you have adults to talk to."

Sunday: As he calls the desk to tell them he is checking out, they inform him his lost luggage is on the way in from the airport.

As he throws up his hands, he inadvertently finds the light switch in the navel of the cherub lamp at his bedside. As he stands in the rain waiting for a cab, a driver splashes mud all over his suit. The doorman says:

"You almost got hit. You're lucky the good Lord is looking after you."

6

"Have a Good Day"

The expression "Have a good day" was born the week our oil supply was depleted, water became scarce, telephone rates went up, gasoline was in short supply, and meat, coffee and sugar prices soared. It was as if the warranty on the country had just expired.

"Have a good day" was something to say.

Ecology became a household word. My husband became a nut on recycling. Until a few years ago he thought recycling was an extra setting on the washer that tore the buttons off his shirts and shredded his underwear. Now, he sits around making towel racks out of oversexed coat hangers.

My daughter poked her head in my kitchen one day and told me my ozone was in trouble.

"Give me a hint," I said. "Has the anti-freeze leaked out of my car? Are my sinus cavities ready to crest? Or did someone flick their Bic near all the papers stored in the basement?"

"I'm talking about aerosol cans," she groaned. "I'm not going to use them anymore and you shouldn't either. Are you aware that Congress is drafting a bill that will include a ban of spray cans using fluorocarbons?"

"I wouldn't have gone so far as to take it to Congress," I said.

"Mother! Surely, you've seen first-hand how the fluorocarbons in pressurized cans can harm the atmospheric layer that screens the sun's radiation."

"You bet," I nodded. "Not to mention what happens when you mistakenly spray tub and tile cleaner on your teeth. I mean, who wants teeth that foam and deodorize?''

''I can't believe it, Mother.'' She smiled. ''Do you realize this is the first meaingful conversation we've been able to carry on in years?''

I passed the bathroom and gave my underarms a spritz with air freshener. These may just be the only two ozones I'll ever get, and I plan to take care of them.

Have a good day. . . .

The more technology the phone company developed, the more complicated using the phone became. I never knew what complicated was until the phone company launched a campaign to save me money.

Everytime I picked up the receiver, I kept seeing the face of an operator on television with half a phone growing out of her ear admonishing, ''Dial direct. Save 60 percent on nights and weekends. Lower rates on shorter distances. Talk one minute to Nashville for twenty-two minutes.''

One Sunday I found myself setting an alarm for 3 A.M. and direct-dialing Nashville to a person I never liked much and talked for four minutes because I saved $1.25. It was a bargain I couldn't afford to pass up. In fact, in four weeks, I saved enough to call my sister in Ohio at a civilized hour during the week with an operator to announce me.

I put up with all of it because I knew communications were moving forward. However, I was totally unprepared one day when an operator from the phone company called to ask if I had made a long distance call to North Carolina, and if so could I supply her with the number I had called as it had not been recorded.

"How did you get my number?" I asked. "It's unlisted."

"From directory assistance," she said.

"Shame on you," I said. "That's an extra. Do you know if you had dialed me on the weekend instead of prime time during the business hours you could have saved thirty-two cents on the first minute?"

"But I . . ."

"Besides, if you call me for assistance three more times this month, you will be charged twenty cents a call. That all adds up. I assume you are calling from a business phone, which is charged full rates, which means each additional minute we talk is costing you forty cents. Frankly, dear, I'm going to do you a big favor and hang up. I don't think you can afford me.''

Have a good day. . . .

The Meat Mutiny came without warning. One day, we were eating more and paying less and the next there were two hundred and seventy-eight products on the market to help our hamburger.

Housewives did not take the news sitting down. They stood outside of grocery stores eating dog food in protest. Signs went up suggesting, FIGHT MEAT PRICES. SUCK YOUR THUMB. And clever cookbooks came out to combat the crisis. (*Cook Cheap* cost $12.95.)

Overnight, butchers became the darlings of the cocktail party, replacing doctors. I hated myself for it, but I found myself playing the game like the rest of the homemakers.

"How's your rump today, Fred," I asked my butcher one day after he called my number.

He looked around cautiously. "You've been a good customer of mine for two years, Erma. Nursed our baby back to health after the flu epidemic and loaned me the money to get my store started. A man doesn't forget things like that. [I smiled.] I can arrange financing on a sirloin tip at 6 percent on the unpaid balance for thirty-six months."

"See you at our house Saturday night?" I smiled.

"You bet," he waved.

I had no shame whatsoever. "Well, if it isn't Fred Sawsil. I hate to bring this up at a social gathering, Fred, but I was wondering if you would prescribe something for a tough round steak. The meat thermometer registers normal and I've already given it two tablespoons of meat tenderizer."

He looked up tiredly. "Take two aspirins and call me in the morning," he said. "Now if you'll excuse me, I have to get back to Mrs. Beeman. She has a sty in the eye of her round."

I stood there in a daze. Somehow, it did

me a world of good just to touch the hand of the man who had touched a standing rib. . . .

Standing at the meat counter day after day was depressing. I found myself looking over cuts of meat that I used to think belonged in bottles at Harvard.

"What is that?" I asked Fred one day. "In the corner of the meat case?"

"Tongue."

"Whose?"

"It was an anonymous donor," he said dryly. "This is tripe," he said, holding up a carton.

"I'll say," I said weakly.

"Have you never tried pig's feet?"

"No, you never know where they've been."

"Chicken?"

"I'll pretend I didn't hear that."

I motioned to Fred to come closer, "Listen, Fred, do you remember that rump roast you financed last week? Well, when you trimmed a little of the fat off it went into deep shock and . . ."

"I don't make house calls," he said stiffly.

"So, why don't you drop over to the house tomorrow," I said, "and I'll have a few people in and. . . ."

"On Wednesdays I play golf," he said.

Have a good day. . . .

I wanted to boycott coffee when it went to four dollars a pound. I really did, but basically I'm weak and cannot endure pain.

I knew I was paying more for three pounds of coffee than I paid for a winter coat when I was first married, but I couldn't help myself.

You cannot imagine the pressure I got from the women in the neighborhood. One morning, I practically ran to the coffee klatsch at Lois's house.

Just inside the door, Lois said, "Want a cup?"

She put an empty cup in my hand.

"Where's the coffee?" I asked.

"I never promised you coffee."

"That's not funny, Lois. Do you have any idea what I would give for a cup of coffee? I'd sell my children."

"Wouldn't we all."

"I'd sell my body."

"Braggart."

"Lois, I'd sell my bowling trophy."

"Will you get hold of yourself? We've got to stand firm together or there's no telling how high the price of coffee will go."

"Look," I said regaining my composure, "I never thought I'd admit this to anyone, but I am older than the rest of you and I lived through the Great Caffeine Drought of 1942 during the war."

"I never heard of it," said Lois.

"And I hope you never do," I said. "I saw my mother in the morning without a cup of coffee once and it's the closest to death I ever want to come. She toasted and buttered her hand and put it on my sister's plate. She bumped into a footstool with her head. She felt a draft and it was her eyelashes blinking. When she thought no one was looking, she put her head in the coffee canister and inhaled. My father caught her trying to shave her tongue. It was awful."

"It must have been a terrible thing for a child to see," comforted Carol, "but courage; it'll all be over soon."

"I know," I whimpered, "but a day without Joe DiMaggio is like a day without sunshine."

You can only be "lousy with courage" for so long. On the way back from the school after lunch, I swung the car into a drive-in and yelled, "One cup of coffee please . . . and will you take a personal check?"

Have a good day. . . .

7

"Warning: Families May Be Dangerous to Your Health"

There's a lot of theories on why the American family is losing ground as an institution.

Some say it's economics . . . others say ecology . . . others blame lack of fulfillment . . . a few opt for priorities, or as one neighbor observed, "Would you want to bring a child into a world that wouldn't elect Ronald Reagan?"

I personally like the American family. It has a lot of potential. Besides, the world is not geared for two people. Twinkies come twelve to a box, kitchen chairs, four to a set, gum, five sticks to the package.

To my way of thinking, the American family started to decline when parents began to communicate with their children. When we began to "rap," "feed into one another," "Let things hang out" that mother didn't know about and would rather not.

Foremost of the villains that ripped the American family to shreds was Education. It was a case of Hide-and-Seek meeting Show and Tell . . . the McGuffey reader crowd locking horns with the Henry Miller group.

The ignorance gap that the new math created between parent and child has not even begun to mend.

Before the new math, I had a mysterious aura about me. I never said anything, but my children were convinced I had invented fire.

When we began to have "input" with one another, my daughter said to me one day, "Mama, what's a variable?"

"It's a weirdo who hangs around the

playground. Where did you read that word? On a restroom wall?"

"It's in my new math book," she said. "I was hoping you could help me. They want me to locate the mantissa in the body of the table and determine the associated antilog ten, and write the characteristics as an exponent on the base of ten."

I thought a minute. "How long has the mantissa been missing?"

She went to her room, locked her door and I never saw her again until after she graduated.

The metric system was no better. Once a child knows that a square millimeter is .00155 square inches, will he ever have respect for a mother who once measured the bathroom for carpeting and found out she had enough left over to slipcover New Jersey?

And what modern-day mother has never been intimidated when she has to communicate with a child's teacher?

I don't think there's anything that makes my morning like a kid looking up from his cereal and saying casually, "I gotta have a note saying I was sick or my teacher won't let me back into school."

"I suppose it has to be written on paper," I ask slumping miserably over the bologna.

"The one you wrote on wax paper she couldn't read. But if you can't find paper, I could stay home for another day," he said.

I tore a piece of wallpaper off the wall and said, "Get me a pencil."

The pencil took a bit of doing. After a fifteen-minute search we finally found a stub in the lint trap of the dryer.

"You sure are whipped up about this note," I sighed.

"You don't understand," he said. "If we don't have one we don't go back to school."

I started to write. "Is your teacher a Miss, a Ms. or a Mrs.?"

"I don't know," he pondered. "She owns her own car and carries her own books."

"Dear Ms. Weems," I wrote.

"On the other hand, she stayed up to watch the Miss America Pageant."

"Dear Miss Weems," I wrote.

"It doesn't matter," he shrugged. "When she has her baby we'll have a new teacher."

"Dear MRS. Weems," I wrote. "Please excuse Brucie from school yesterday. When he awoke in the morning he complained of stomach cramps and . . ."

"Cross out stomach cramps," he ordered, "tell her I was too sick to watch TV."

"Dear Mrs. Weems, Brucie had the urgencies and . . ."

"What does urgencies mean?"

"Stomach cramps."

"Don't tell her that! The last time you wrote that she put me next to the door and didn't take her eyes off me all day long."

"It was your imagination," I said. "Do you need a note or not?"

"I told you I can't go to school without it."

"Okay then, get me the dictionary and turn to the D's."

He looked over my shoulder. "What does D-I-A-R-R-H-E-A mean?"

"It means you sit by the door again," I said, licking the envelope.

Composing the note took twenty-five minutes, which was eight minutes longer than the signing of the Declaration of Independence. I wouldn't bring it up, but only yesterday I was cleaning out a jacket pocket and there was the note: unread and unnecessary.

To me, modern education is a contradiction. It's like a three-year-old kid with a computer in his hand who can multiply 10.6 percent interest of $11,653, but doesn't know if a dime is larger or smaller than a nickel.

It is like your daughter going to college and taking all your small appliances, linens, beddings, furniture, luggage, TV set and car and then saying, "I've got to get away from your shallow materialism."

My kids always talk a great game of ecology. Yet, they harbor the No. 1 cause of pollution in this country: gym clothes.

A pair of shorts, a shirt and a pair of gym shoes walked into the utility room under their own steam last Wednesday and leaned helplessly against the wall. I stood there while I watched a pot of ivy shrivel and die before my eyes.

Blinking back the tears, I yelled to my son, "How long has it been since these clothes have been washed?"

"Since the beginning of the school year," he shouted back.

"What school year?"

"1972-1973."

"I thought so. You know, I don't know how your P.E. teacher stands it."

"He said we weren't too bad until yesterday."

"What happened yesterday?"

"It rained and we came inside."

"Don't you have rules about laundering these things?"

"Yeah. We have to have them washed every four months whether they need it or not."

Carefully, I unfolded the muddy shorts, the brittle T-shirt and the socks that were already in the final stages of rigor mortis.

As I tried to scrape off a French fry entangled in a gym shoestring, I couldn't help but reflect that this was a child who had been reared in an antiseptic world.

When he was a baby, I used to boil his toys and sterilize his navel bands. I made the dog wear a mask when he was in the same room. I washed my hands BEFORE I changed his diapers.

Where had I failed?

Under his bed were dirty clothes that were harboring wildlife. In his drawers were pairs of soiled underwear so old that some had plastic liners in them. His closet had overalls and jeans that hung suspended without the need of hangers.

Opening the lid of the washer, I felt around trying to find the gym clothes that I had just washed. I retrieved a shoestring, two labels and a clean French fry.

"What happened to my gym clothes?" asked my son.

"After the sweat and dirt went, this was all that was left."

Probably the most blatant contradiction between what a child is at home and what he is at school manifests itself at the annual Athletic Banquet.

Next time you attend an athletic awards banquet, catch the look on the faces of mothers as the accomplishments of their sons and daughters are revealed. It is as if they are talking about a different person with the same name as your youngster.

By intense concentration, you can sometimes read the parents' thoughts, as the coaches pay them homage.

"Mark is probably one of the best sprinters I've had in my entire career here at So. High. Hang onto your hats, people. Mark ran the hundred-yard dash in nine point nine!"

(Had to be nine days and nine hours. I once asked him to run out the garbage and it sat by the sink until it turned into a bookend.)

"I don't know what the baseball team would do without Charlie. We've had chatterers on the team before who get the guys whipped up, but Charlie is the all-time chatterer. There isn't a moment when he isn't saying something to spark the team."

(Charlie speaks six words to me in a week. "When you going to the store?")

"For those of you who don't really understand field events, I want to explain about the shotput. It's a ball weighing eight pounds that was thrown a hundred feet by an outstanding athlete here at So. . . . Wesley Whip.''

(That's funny. Wesley looks like the same boy who delivers my paper and can't heave a six-ounce Saturday edition all the way from his bike to my porch.)

"Wolf Man Gus will go down in football annals as one of the all-time greats here at So. High. In the game with Central, Gus scored the winning touchdown despite a chipped bone in his ankle, a dislocated shoulder and a fever of a hundred and two.''

(So how come Wolf Man Gus stays home from school every time he has his teeth cleaned?)

"I don't suppose anyone has better reflexes in this entire state than our outstanding basketball rebounder, Tim Rim. When the Good Lord passed out coordination, Tim was first in line.''

(Tim is seventeen years old and I can still only pour him a half-glass of milk because that's all I want to clean up.)

"Tennis is a gentleman's game. This

year's recipient of the Court Courtesy award is none other than So. High's Goodwill Ambassador, Stevie Cool."

(He's certainly come a long way since he tried to break his brother's face last week when he took a record album without asking.)

"The swimming team would never have made it this year without our plucky little manager, Paul Franswarth. Paul picks up those wet towels off the floor, hangs up the suits to dry, and is responsible for putting all the gear back where it belongs."

(Let's go home, Ed. I feel sick.)

It seems the more I talk with my children, the less I understand them. Take the subject of Coed Dorms.

Of all the changes parents have had to adjust to, coed dorms has probably been one of the most difficult to understand. Some dormitories have even conducted parent - student seminars where the student explains patiently, "We need a freer atmosphere where boys and girls come to know one another as friends, rather than sex objects," and the father of a freshman daughter laments, "That can't be done in a coffee shop?"

I was against coed dorms from the beginning. Not because it was a sensuous supermarket, but because I felt if anyone ever saw my son's bedroom in its natural state, I'd never get the kid married off and now my worst fears have been realized.

At Stanford, male and female students (although not given permission by the school) are using the same bathrooms. Take my word, when you see a man dribbling toothpaste and hair into a washbowl each morning and gargling like someone just pulled the plug on Lake Erie, love goes right out the window.

I know the trend is for young people to go the frankness and honesty route, but premarital clutter could stamp out marriages forever.

Men! Could you establish a meaningful relationship with a girl who put an angora sweater to dry on your last bath towel? Can you shave in a room full of steam with your face framed in a dripping pair of pantyhose? Do your really want to know how often she has to shave her legs? Could you ever be important enough to a girl to have her take the rollers out of her hair? (I swear I saw a teenage bride at her own wedding with her hair in rollers. When I asked her why she said, "We might go somewhere afterward.")

Women! Could you have a meaningful relationship with a boy who entered school in September with thirty-eight pairs of sweat sox and is just getting around to asking where the Laundromat is? Could you afford a man who uses a can of deodorant a day under each arm? Who belches before breakfast and hangs his trousers under the mattress?

As my house mother once told me when I was in college, "There is nothing that attracts the opposite sex like a busy signal . . . a locked door . . . and the word 'No.' If you want a friend . . . buy a dog."

According to the experts, if we didn't talk to our children and appreciate them every minute of the day, when they were gone we would sit in a recliner with a phone in our lap and hum all day long.

There isn't a mother alive who has not lived in dreaded terror of "The Empty Nest."

It was a long time in coming. First, you had to get the child out of bed and into a line of work.

For kids who are the most educated, well-read, best-informed people in the world, their attitude toward work is not to be believed. Next to an oarsman on a slave ship whose captain wanted to water ski, the most maligned person on the face of this earth is the teenager who has just landed his first full-time job.

No one suffers more and is appreciated less.

My son considers himself a "human sacrifice on the altar of the Church of the Establishment." He was fifteen before we could use the word "employment" in front of him. The word broke his face out and he preferred we spell it. The way he explained it to us on the eve of his marriage to a paycheck, "This is an exercise in group persecution, isn't it? All of you have run the course and now before

I come of age, I have to prove that I can hack the nine-to-five number, is that it? Okay, you win. If I have to prove that I'm mature, I'll get the dumb full-time J-O-B . . . jjjj . . . jjjooo . . . jjjjjoooooob!''

Maybe a lot of you know my son . . . or at least have heard of him.

He's the only employed person who has to work all day and then come home and feed himself.

He's the only dedicated teenager in North America to work when the ''gang'' went tubing down the river one Wednesday afternoon.

He's the first person to ever have half of his paycheck withheld for some service that he has never requested (federal income tax, hospitalization, social security, etc.). As he stated, ''Someone is going to hear about this.''

He stands alone as the only worker who is dominated by a senile boss (age thirty-five) who engages in office brutality by insisting he arrive on time in the mornings and after lunch.

He's the only full-time worker in the country who has not gained the respect of

104

family and friends for his contribution to labor.

Last Saturday, I tapped him on the shoulder, "Hey, George Meany, out of the sack. It's the crack of noon."

My son rolled over. "I do not believe this is happening to a working person," he said. "All week long, I work five days a week, eight hours a day and what do I get for it?"

"You get all your meals served like a sultan, your bedroom cleaned, your clothes washed and ironed and a full-time old family retainer . . . me!"

Something tells me I'll have the first kid to retire three years before he has anything to retire from.

Once employment is attained, however, you are for the first time in your life . . . alone at last. The family structure as you knew it will never be the same again.

You have weathered loose teeth, stolen bikes, team teaching, bunk beds, baton twirling, G.I. Joe, Driver's Ed., lost billfolds, Sunday night term papers, the draft, and the Doobie Brothers.

Cue the recliner and the phone . . . the

Empty Nest sequence is about to begin.

As I walked into my son's empty room, I felt I was in the presence of a shrine.

Everything was intact, just as he left it. I fondled the sherbet glass with the petrified pudding under his bed . . . ran my fingers lovingly over his drum that leaked oil on the carpet . . . and cried softly as I tiptoed around the mounds of dirty underwear that didn't fit him anymore.

I made plans to preserve the room as a living memorial where I could go in the heat of the day and be by myself and reflect on the past.

Then one day as I meditated, I noticed he had an entire wall with nothing on it, so I moved the pump organ from the hallway into his bedroom. Noting the light was pretty good in his room, I also discovered by moving out his drums and storing them I could put my sewing machine in the corner with a table for cutting.

As we were making the change, my husband observed there was an entire closet free, so why shouldn't he move his clothes into the closet? By discarding five years of *Sports Illustrated* my son had saved, we found room for the Christmas decorations and the carton of canceled checks.

More and more of the family began to visit the "Temple." It became a haven for camping gear, pictures that needed framing, storage for summer lawn furniture and newspapers awaiting recycling.

The shelf of tennis trophies gave way to a supply of bleach bottles to be used by the women of the church for a project, the chest of drawers for my bicycle exerciser, and the bed was moved out of the room to create space — stored to make way for a rocker and a TV set.

Naturally, the walls were too masculine for the room, so we painted them yellow and slipcovered the rocker in a bright pink and orange.

Just before Christmas, there was a knock on the door. It was our son home for a visit.

"Hey, long time no see," said my husband. "Son of a gun. How long can you stay? Terrific. We've still got the old sofa bed in the den and you're welcome to it as long as you like.''

This morning, my husband said, ''How long is your relative going to stay?''

''My relative!'' I shrugged. ''I thought he was YOURS.''

8

There Ought to Be a Law . . .

When in the course of human events, one's sanity is in jeopardy, it becomes necessary for a lone voice in the wilderness to cry out.

It is in the name of justice for all . . . but especially me . . . that I offer the following declarations that would provide peace of mind for so many.

A Baby's Bill of Rights

Article the first: People who chew garlic shall not be allowed within three miles of a baby under penalty of drowning by spitting.

Article the second: Excessive bail shall be set for turkeys who tickle a baby's feet until he faints, or throw him up in the air after a full meal.

Article the third: Where a crime of the kidneys has been committed, the accused should enjoy the right to a speedy diaper change. Public announcements, details and guided tours of the aforementioned are not necessary.

Article the fourth: The decision to eat strained lamb or not to eat strained lamb should be with the "feedee" and not the "feeder." Blowing the strained lamb into the feeder's face should be accepted as an opinion, not as a declaration of war.

Article the fifth: Babies should enjoy the freedom to vocalize, whether it be in church, a public meeting place, during a movie, or after hours when the lights are out. They have not yet learned that joy and laughter have to last a lifetime and must be conserved.

Amendment one: No baby shall at any time be quartered in a house where there are no soft laps, no laughter, or no love.

The Hernia Amendment to the National Anthem

Few will argue that the inspirational words of Francis Scott Key are stirring enough to make Jane Fonda enlist in the Coast Guard. But something has got to be done about the melody of our national anthem before someone hurts himself.

I watched a man at the ball game the other Sunday standing tall and proud as he sang, "Oh say can you see." But by the time he got to the high-pitched, "And the rockets' red glare," the veins were standing out in his neck, his face became flushed and his voice cracked like Andy Hardy asking the Judge for the keys to the Packard.

Sensing I was looking at him, he gasped and said "I love this country."

"Me too," I said sadly, stuffing a program in his mouth.

You take your average citizen. He sings on maybe ten or twelve occasions a year and does not have what is normally called your "trained voice." He can make

"Happy Birthday to Marvin" (if they start low) or "Should Auld Acquaintance Be Forgot" and maybe a chorus of the "Beer Barrel Polka" with a few beers, but beyond that he is limited.

Me? It is my experience that everytime I go from the "twilight's last gleaming" to "the ramparts we watched" there is pain on the inside of my right leg, so I do everyone a favor by just mouthing the words. Invariably, everywhere I go, I am seated next to Beverly Sills, who comes down on "land of the free" with two notes. (The latter reached only the ears of a springer spaniel in New England.)

As I was setting down these thoughts I wondered who wrote the music to "The Star-Spangled Banner" and went to my reference book. Ironically, the music was an old English drinking song called "To Anacreon in Heaven." (Obviously, the drunks could sing the melody, but they had trouble with Anacreon.)

I personally believe there are a lot of patriotic Americans around who would like to sing "The Star-Spangled Banner" in its entirety, but who are discriminated against because they are bluebirds (singers with a range of one octave).

Would it be unreal to have one national anthem with two melodies? One for the traditionalists who can also sing Bacharach's "Alfie" without fainting, and a simple tune for those of us who sing in the cracks in the piano?

To the 3,085 ball players who chew tobacco, this could mean a lot.

Kissing by
Mutual Ratification

This country has to make a hard-and-fast rule about greeting people with a kiss.

Either we all are, or we all aren't. Frankly, I gave up kissing people hello at the age of seven when my mother hired a piano teacher who chewed garlic. It was enough to make you do the *Minute Waltz* in ten seconds.

It wasn't until I began appearing on talk shows that I saw the return of the kissy-kissy. It was weird. The same persons who kissed you when you walked into the studio, also kissed you when you returned from the makeup room, the green room, and the ladies room. Not only that, but when you saw them again on the set, they acted like they hadn't seen you since World War I when they left you for dead in Paris with the fever.

Actually, kissing people hello takes some skill. First, you have to establish who is going to be the kisser and who is going to be the kissee. There should be no indecision once the kisser has decided to plant one on. He or she should grab the kissee by either the hands or the shoulders and kiss from the left (only vampires approach from the right).

If you are kissing another woman, beware of earrings that will strike you blind, jewelry that can puncture the inflated parts of your body and instant asphyxiation in a nest of stiff hair. (I was once speared and deflated by an open pin on a name card that said, "Hello, My Name Is Inez Funkhouser.")

Of prime consideration is the length of the kiss. What is considered good taste for a kiss of greeting? I have seen producers greet guests in such an enthusiastic way that I can only assume (a) he was giving mouth-to-mouth resuscitation to a dead woman or (b) they are leaving after the show to pick out the dishes.

A hello-greeting should be a quick, impersonal peck with all the passion of a sex-starved orangutan. Some kissers are so casual that while they are pecking you, their eyes are picking out the next kissee.

The person who is far-sighted encounters other problems in the kissing custom. I once embraced a water cooler for five minutes while insisting, "What do you mean I don't remember you, Florence?"

It is generally acknowledged that one woman kissing another, especially when she sees her all the time, is "senseless."

As I said the other day when I kissed a man with a toothpick in his mouth, "Ouch."

Search and Seizure Rights in the Laundry Room

I tacked a note up in the utility room yesterday that read, **"All clothes left here over ninety days will be towed away at the owner's expense and sold at public auction."**

"What does that mean?" asked my youngest.

"It means you have diapers at the bottom of your stack of clothes and you are thirteen years old. It means I am sick of watching you dress each morning over the toaster. It means your clothes have a home and I want to see them in that home."

"I've been meaning to talk with you about that," he said. "Why did you throw my blue jeans in the wash?"

"Because they were in the middle of the floor."

"Were they scrunched down to two little holes?"

I nodded. "What's that got to do with it?"

116

"When they're scrunched down like that, they aren't dirty."

"So, how am I supposed to know when they are dirty?"

"The dirty ones are kicked under the bed."

"Why don't you put them on top of the bed?"

"Because I don't want to get them mixed up with the clean clothes."

"Instead of sleeping with your clean clothes, why don't you take them out of the laundry room and put them in a drawer?"

"Because that's where I keep the dirty underwear I am going to wear again."

I took a deep breath. "Why would you wear underwear two days in a row?"

"Because it is my lucky underwear."

"For whom?" I asked dryly.

"I suppose you want me to put my clothes in the clothes hamper?" he asked.

"It crossed my mind."

"With all the wet towels in there my clothes would get ruined."

"You are supposed to put your wet towels on the towel rack."

"What'll I do with all your pantyhose and sweaters?"

"PUT THEM IN THE UTILITY ROOM," I shouted.

"Does this mean I lose my place dressing over the toaster?" he asked.

I planted a firm hand on his bottom. "No, it means your underwear just got unlucky."

Regulation of Interstate Shopping Cart Traffic

It is my feeling that the driving age of shoppers operating supermarket carts be raised to thirty-five. Going to the supermarket used to be an adventure. Today, it's a combat mission.

As I was telling a friend the other day, "It's a jungle out there what with all the young, inexperienced drivers and little old ladies who only drive a shopping cart on Sundays after church.

The shopping cart is the most underrated traffic hazard on the road today. To begin with, no license is required in any state to drive these little vehicles. Anyone, regardless of age, vision, physical condition or mental health can get behind the wheels. (Occasionally, no one is behind the wheels, and these little irresponsible devils slam into cars in the parking lot without a driver in sight.)

To say that they are unsafe at any speed is an understatement. Consider, if you will, their deficiencies.

1. *Grocery carts are never parked. They are welded together as a group at the door and must be separated by kicking, jiggling, wiggling, and a good stiff kick in the old breadbasket. This possibly accounts for the body construction being weakened. (Yours, not the cart.)*

2. *A safety check would reveal there isn't a shopping cart that does not have all four wheels working. Unfortunately, all four are locked in stable directions. Three wheels want to shop and the fourth wants to go to the parking lot.*

3. *There are no seat belts for the*

children riding in shopping cart seats. Thus, it is not unusual to have them lean into your cart and eat half-a-pound of raw hamburger before you discover they are there.

4. *Shopping carts should be like airplanes and nuns . . . it takes two to handle the situation. One to drive and one to gawk and read the caloric content of frozen lasagna.*

5. *Passing in the supermarket is hazardous because supermarket aisles are built to accommodate the width of one-and-one-half carts. Thus, we encourage the reckless driver who fears the whipped cream topping in his cart is melting and who will purposely force your cart into produce.*

And here's the shocker. There are no brakes on a shopping cart.

And what is worse . . . Ralph Nader doesn't even care.

Truth in
Fair Packaging of
Children

We do a lot of talking in this country about "fair packaging." People like to know what they are getting before they get stuck with it.

I do a lot of thinking about how I am going to merchandise my kids. Frankly, in clear conscience, I don't see how I can let them go into marriage without slapping a sticker on their foreheads that reads: "This Person May Be Injurious to Your Mental Health."

I have visions of some poor bride coming to me in tears and saying, "You tricked me. Why didn't you tell me your son doesn't know how to close a door after himself."

It will only be a matter of time before she discovers he is lacking in other basic skills and I will feel guilty. For example, my son does not know how to wring out a washcloth. I have held washcloth seminars in which I have demonstrated the twist-wrist action. He still insists on dropping it sopping full of water wherever he happens to be standing.

He cannot fold a newspaper after he has read it, hear a phone ring unless it is for him, put a cap on a bottle or tube, or carry on a conversation unless his mouth is full.

He hangs his clothes on a chair, has a three-months' supply of snacks hidden in his desk drawer and makes his bed by smoothing it over with a coat hanger.

Unless he changes drastically, he will be impossible to live with. He insists on having his own window in the car, calling seconds on the meat before he sits down at the table, and once confessed to a friend he does not brush his teeth until school starts in September.

No, I would be a traitor to my own sex if I did not put a tag around this child's neck reading: Boy. Eleven years old. Made in U.S.A. Height, 4'8'', net weight (including package) seventy-six pounds. Natural coloring, blond in summer, washed out in winter.

Capacity: Eight meals a day. Contains

thirty-five hundred calories at all times. Artifically sweetened.

Unaffected by sun, rain and mud. Standard ingredients: 80 percent charm, 10 percent goldbricking and 1 percent energy.

Read label carefully. Take eleven-year-old boy with tongue-in-cheek, grain of salt, and a frequent checkup.

Constitutionality of Drive-in Windows

It's just my own personal observation, but I don't think God ever meant for man to do his banking, order food, or mail a letter from the driver's seat of the car.

I have noted only two cars that have swung precariously up to the position where they can comfortably do business. One was a car from a demolition derby and the other was a rental. Neither had anything to lose.

Drive-in banks intimidate me the most, possibly because I am "on camera" and quite self-conscious about having the tellers gather and exclaim, "Watch this one, Dorothy. She's the one who fell apart when her fender was ripped off last week."

Consequently, I have become something of a conservative. I pull in a good six feet from the window and when the drawer slides out I find that by opening my car door and forcing my head through my shoulder seat belt, pushing on the brake pedal with my right foot and bending my knee against the gearshift for leverage, I can slide my deposit slip into the drawer providing (a) I discontinue breathing for a while and (b) there are no high winds to circulate my deposit slip in the parking lot.

The mailboxes are something else. I never pull up to one of them that I don't visualize a meeting of the postal department in Washington figuring out how to position the boxes.

"No, no, Chester," says the designer. "You have placed the boxes on the driver's side of the car. We mustn't pamper them. Put them on the passenger side so the driver will have to put the car in park, straddle the stick shift in the console, cup his throat over the window and just try to sail the letter into this six-inch slot.''

''Then the slot should be just above the pick-up times that have become blurred and unreadable?'' asked Chester.

''Higher, Chester, much higher,'' smiled his boss.

Yelling an order for five into a clown's mouth is something else again. Especially when you are alone. I feel like such a fool shouting until the varicose veins in my neck surface.

As my husband observed, ''You don't have to go to drive-ins, you know. You can always use your feet.''

Better to grow long arms.

Are Family Vacations Legal?

So many parents have been the victims of family vacations it is just possible that many of them are not familiar with some existing laws on how to handle some of

125

the crises that arise. These are some of the most common inquiries:

THE ABANDON-CHILD LAW

It is illegal in forty-seven states to leave a child in a rest room and pretend it was a mistake. Maryland and Utah are sympathetic to parents if they can produce a doctor's certificate showing mental deterioration caused by the trip. Alaska (which is quite permissive) allows a mild sedation for the children.

THE NEW JERSEY vs KIDDER LAW

It is illegal on the New Jersey turnpike for a child to hang out of the car window and make a noise like a siren. A decision on this was handed down in 1953, after forty-five cars (including three police cruisers) pulled over to the side of the road and tied up traffic for fifty-two hours.

THE KEY DECISION

All fifty states have rulings regarding children who collect rest room keys as souvenirs. One of the stiffer penalties is feeding a child a quart of Gatorade and putting him outside a locked door until the key shows up.

THE NO-FAULT LITTER LAW

Vehicles bearing families are not permitted to stop in the downtown area of cities having populations of four hundred and fifty thousand or more to look for a gym shoe that someone threw out of the moving vehicle. It is suggested that mothers put name tapes and full addresses on both shoes.

ANTI-NOISE LAWS

Nearly every city (including three ghost towns in Arizona) has the noise-pollutant law. If, in fact your vacationers have two radios playing at full volume, a barking dog and a father screaming, "Would anyone believe we didn't HAVE to get married," and can be heard with all the car windows up, everyone in the car can be arrested.

SAFE DRIVING LAW

It is unlawful to inflate a twenty-foot life raft in a sedan blocking Daddy's view of the road, braid his hair while he is driving in the mountains, or tie his shoes together when he is going through a tunnel.

PRIVILEGED CONVERSATION

Conversation heard over CB radios and messages on rest-room walls repeated by children should not be grounds for shooting a child's tongue full of Novocaine unless such child dwells on same for several miles.

REGAINING SINGLE STATUS ON AN EXIT RAMP

This is tricky, but some parents have opted to dissolve a family relationship on the spot by summoning legal aid. In this event, however, it is well to remember that children get custody of the station wagon.

Illegal Possession of Junk Food

A grade school principal in the East became so upset about the lack of nutrition in the lunches the children were eating, that he declared an edict banning junk food from the cafeteria.

I have a feeling the kids jammed the edict between two potato chips and two squares of Hershey chocolate and had it for lunch.

There is certainly no quarrel with the theory. Children should eat nutritionally balanced meals. But children do not take to ultimatums. I would have tried the old Accentuate-the-negative-reverse-the-positive-and-make-the-kid-think-your-idea-is-his-and-he's-driving-you-crazy approach.

Instead of an edict, the bulletin would

have read something like this:

Memo to: School Children
Re: Nutritional Lunches

1. *Carrots are illegal on school premises. Children bringing them from home will need a note from a parent giving permission to have them, or they will be confiscated by the office and held until dismissal time.*

2. *Locker inspection for thermoses containing hot vegetable soup or other nutritious dishes will be held periodically without warning. At that time, students are instructed to go to their lockers and stand at attention. DO NOT UNLOCK YOUR LOCKER UNTIL A TEACHER INSTRUCTS YOU TO DO SO. Thermoses will be destroyed by the custodian.*

3. *Because of student demand, we are selling fresh fruit by the door in the cafeteria. This is on a trial basis. If we find this is all students are having for lunch it will be discontinued. Remember, the fruit contains sugar and Billy Tooth is watching you. To*

130

avoid congestion at fruit counter, please have correct change.

4. Teachers have reported to the office that raisin boxes and milk cartons have been found on the school grounds. We know there are students who have been sneaking nutritious foods on the premises and for this reason students have been posted and are instructed to "take names."

5. Your principal will be patrolling the lunchroom where he wants to see potato chips, candy bars, tortilla chips, soft drinks and ice cream. Remember, junk foods build soft bones, soft teeth and make you sleep a lot.

Trust me, it will work.

The Right to Declare War

I read the other day where a body that was believed to be dead was recovered from Lake Michigan. When it warmed up considerably, thaw set in and the person was alive.

Big deal.

Thanks to well-meaning merchants who set their refrigeration at wax museum temperatures, I am in a solidified state from May to September. No one even notices.

I go to a movie carrying a coat over my arm. I go to the supermarket and spend half my time warming my hands on the rotisserie. I drive my car on the wrong side of the street just to get a patch of sun on my arm. The other night at an intimate little restaurant, I said to my husband halfway through dinner, "Would you put your arm around me?"

"You wanta make love or you wanta eat?" he asked, buttering a piece of garlic bread.

"It's nothing personal," I said. "I'm freezing to death. Can you see anyone around us?"

"Not too well," he said, squinting into the darkness. "Why?"

"If everyone else is hanging from hooks, maybe we got into the food locker by mistake."

"I'm perfectly comfortable," he said, snuggling into his wool sport coat.

"Maybe you're anemic or something. You should go to a doctor if you're cold all the time."

In the doctor's office, the nurse smiled and said, "Hello."

"That's easy for you to say," I grumbled; "you're wearing a sweater."

She showed me into a room where she instructed me, "Take off your clothes and slip into this." I put on a paper gown with a back exit big enough to drive a truck through and slid onto the cold metal table. I was shivering uncontrollably when the doctor came in, took a stethoscope out of the refrigerator, and placed it on my chest. I blew on my hands and coughed.

He stood up slowly, removed the stethoscope from around his neck and walked slowly to his desk. "If I didn't know better, I'd think you were dead."

"What gave me away?" I asked.

"The tear in your eye when my breathing steamed up your glasses."

Register Camera Nuts

You will understand me when as a woman who is married to an amateur camera freak, I respectfully suggest that some kind of legislation be passed requiring a permit to carry a loaded camera.

I don't mean to overreact, but I live in fear that someday my husband will point that thing at me, forget he has taken off the lens cap, and click click! I'll end up another statistic at Fotomat.

I have been photographed walking out of a public bathhouse in a Michigan campground wearing a nightgown, curlers, and rain slicker . . . fishing around in my mouth with my fingers trying to remove a fishbone . . . and there are thirty prints floating around somewhere of me on my side in a bathing suit, that I would give up my next unborn child to get the negatives of.

The other day my husband was flipping the camera around carelessly when I said irritably, "Is that thing loaded?"

"Look," he said, "how many accidents have I had with this camera?"

"There was the time you snapped Fred at the office Christmas party trying to Xerox Miss Frampton. He threatened to rearrange your nose. Then, there was the time exposure when you nearly broke your leg trying to get back into the picture . . . and the birthday party where . . ."

"All right, so join the camera lobby and try to get them off the market."

All I'm saying is cameras shouldn't be made available to the man on the street . . . only professionals who know how to use them. The way it stands now, any child can walk right into a camera store and buy a Sunday afternoon special right off the counter . . . no questions asked. The next thing you know some innocent person is staring into the eye of an Instamatic.

"C'mon, you're making a big deal over nothing. I don't use the camera all that much. I just feel kind of important when I have a camera riding back there in the window of my pickup truck. Besides, it's sorta fun watching people's reactions when you point it at them."

He grabbed the camera and trained it

on my hips, which look like I'm carrying two U.S. mail pouches for the pony express. I heard the button click.

"Fooled you. The camera isn't loaded."

One of these days he will push me too far. And there isn't a woman jury in this country who would find me guilty.

9

"Gametime"

The other morning I watched five game shows in a row on television. I wanted to turn them off, but I was too mesmerized by the contestants.

The first one was a frail woman who said "I am a simple, average housewife," then proceeded to win a toaster by humming the fight song of Bangladesh High.

The second one said she was a mother of seven, then spewed out the fuel formula for the Russian Soyuz XI space flight last year.

The third was also a "typical, suburban homemaker," who won a year's supply of tulip bulbs by answering that the Sixth

Crusade in Europe was led by Frederick II in 1228. (I thought it was Billy Graham in 1965.)

After I flipped off the TV set, I sat there stunned for a minute. Not only could I not remember what I had for breakfast three hours before, but I realized that mentally I had let myself go to pot.

I prattled on at cocktail parties about Jacqueline Onassis traveling with four silk sheets, and how David Cassidy got a hickey on prom night.

My vocabulary had dwindled to three Buckley-type words: Erudite (meaning smart), which I didn't use for years because it sounded dirty. Deciduous (to lose one's leaves), which I read off a tree at the Garden Center. And noxious, which I overheard my ten year old use to describe my casserole. (I think it means you can't get it without a prescription.)

At card club, I broached the subject, "How in the world do those women on game shows do it?"

"They fake it," said Gloria. "Anyone can go on an intellectual crash program and change their image in five days."

"Like how?" I asked.

"First, put copies of the *London Times Literary Supplement* in your bathroom. That's status. Then when you go to the beauty shop, take a stack of books along and run your fingers across the lines as fast as you can turn the pages. Everyone will think you're a graduate of Evelyn Wood's speed-reading course.

"When you're in a crowded room, look perplexed and say in a loud voice, "Archie Bunker? Who publishes him?" Confide to the town gossip that you had to buy a truss in order to carry the Sunday New York *Times* around.

"And above all, put together a group of one-liners for dinner parties such as, "Isn't it incredulous that there would be fifty-seven-million, ninety-three-thousand United States dollars in circulation last year and I cannot find thirty-five-cents for a school lunch in the mornings?"

"I don't know, Gloria," I said, "I still can't figure out how this housewife knew about Frederick II in 1228."

"Just a lucky guess," said Gloria.

"Look," said Jackie, throwing in her

hand, "let me give you a piece of advice. "Don't get hooked on game shows. I once watched game shows every day for a week. I began with the 'Gong Show' right after breakfast and didn't stir from in front of the set until 'To Tell the Truth' went off at seven-thirty.

"By this time I had undergone a complete personality change. I saw Nipsy Russell everywhere . . . I wanted a five-piece dinette set for remembering my own name. I pushed imaginary buzzers and shouted out for no apparent reason, 'I'll bet twenty dollars on the red.'

"Dinner was a challenge. I couldn't remember if it was door No. 1 (the oven) door No. 2 (the freezer) or door No. 3 (the cupboard). Also I couldn't seem to be able to concentrate on what anyone was saying. I'd just smile and mumble, 'I want to come back tomorrow and try for the car.'

"One game, 'Break Up a Marriage,' intrigued me. You know, it's the game where a wife tries to answer the questions the way she thinks her husband will answer and vice versa. Actually, it's a shortcut to World War III. When my husband came home I had to know, 'What would you say would be the most embarrassing moment at our wedding?'

" 'When our kids showed up.'

" 'Isn't that just like you to be cute when there are His and Her Motorbikes riding on an answer?'

" 'Okay, if you want a straight answer, when your mother arrived at the wedding in a hearse, wearing a black veil.'

" 'Maybe we'd better get it all out in the open.'

" 'Yeah, well, maybe I should give you more room.'

" 'That's terrible,' I said.

"It's turning out all right," she said. "Next week we're both contestants on a new show, 'Trial Separation.' "

Despite what Gloria and Jackie said, I still have nothing but admiration for the men and women who compete on these shows. Every week the games seem to get more involved, the prizes more fabulous and the contestants more frenzied.

I have seen these poor housewife-contestants run the emotional yo-yo from hysterical to rabid. Frankly, I don't know how much longer they can continue under the strain. For example, I watched a new game show last week that was called simply "CORONARY." It was relatively simple to follow.

A contestant was asked to select a number that corresponded to a balloon. When she broke it, a little card fell out telling her what she had won. It went something like this.

"Hang on, Bernice," said the moderator. "Do you know what you have just won?" Bernice shakes her head numbly. "You have won one hundred and twenty-five thousand dollars."

As the band plays "Happy Days Are Here Again," Bernice jumps fifteen feet off the floor and throws her arms around the moderator's neck and begins to weep uncontrollably.

He holds up his hand for silence. "In Italian lira, Bernice. Do you know how much that is in American money? About forty-eight dollars and twelve cents. Too bad, Bernice, but wait! You are going to pick up the lira in an Italian bank. You have won three weeks in Rome!"

Bernice clutches her chest and sways dizzily as the band starts up again. She grabs the moderator's sleeve.

"That's Rome, New York." He grins.

Bernice slumps again, emotionally drained.

"But wait! Look what you'll be wearing to New York." The curtain opens to reveal a four-thousand-dollar mink coat. The moderator helps her put it on. Bernice manages a weak smile and a wave to the audience.

"Unfortunately, it's not your size. Too bad, Bernice, had it fit you you would have walked out of here in a four-thousand-dollar mink coat with a Swiss bank account for one hundred thousand dollars in the pocket."

Bernice faints dead away on the floor. The moderator bends over her. "You didn't stay conscious, Bernice. Those are the rules, but since you've been a sport, no one goes away empty-handed. For your consolation prize, we have a personalized pacemaker . . . let's hear it for Bernice."

The way I see it, it's only a matter of

time before game-show contestants will turn pro. Naturally, they'll have to pass a complete physical indicating they are up to the pressures of competition. And they'll probably all be graduates of the Jubilance and Excitement Training schools, which will chain all over the country. Their brochure will undoubtedly go something like this.

Joe Carter's Jubilance and Excitement Seminar

WHO IS ELIGIBLE?

Persons over eighteen years of age who can pass the grueling physical requirements: (a) jumping higher than Bob Barker's head; (b) ignoring the symptoms of a coronary when you have just won a trip to Athens, Georgia, and not Greece; (c) sitting four hours under a barrage of hot lights, dressed as a battery, until called upon by Monty Hall, and still becoming hysterical.

144

CURRICULUM — WHIMPERING AND QUIVERING (3 credit hours)

A "must" for contestants to employ between the time they've answered the question and the time they've found out what they've won. It includes biting your lip until it bleeds, wringing hands, listening to the audience shout obscenities and rolling eyes back in head until whites are showing.

WHAT TO DO WHEN YOU'VE WON THE CAR (5 credit hours)

An in-depth study in hysteria taught by the winner of a 1953 Chevy who won it by knowing Gentle Ben's nickname.

HUGGING AND KISSING TV GAME SHOW HOSTS NEED NOT BE FATAL (3 credit hours)

Pressure points around the throat, cutting off breathing with your body, and lifting host off the floor are outlined.

WHAT TO DO WHEN
THE CHEST PAINS COME

Know which shows have oxygen and which ones expect you to be a sport about a coronary. Remember, there is no jubilance and excitement in passing out. Learn how to stay on your feet.

LOOK LIKE A LOSER TO THE IRS

Handy tips on how to stagger by the IRS men carrying a bag of gold and still hang on to your citizenship.

Remember, game shows can hurt you. Be a pro!

What a shame. It'll be too late for Bernice.

10

Fashions and Fads That Underwhelmed Me

You always hear about fashion's success stories.

How a starlet lost an earring one night and by the next morning, the entire country was wearing one earring. Or how sweaters made a comeback in a drugstore, or a First Lady influenced how we dressed during her reign.

But what about the losers? The fashions that came in and went out the same day? The hopes and dreams of designers that were shattered by the sound of fifty million women . . . laughing themselves to death.

Some styles, for one reason or another, just don't make it.

Remember the Scratch and Smell T-shirt? This should have been a smash. The principle was great. You scratched and voilà . . . a scent was circulated that ran the gamut from perfume to pizza. Unfortunately, there were too many impostors. People scratched for status and stirred up only perspiration. This gave the official scratch and smell shirt a bad name . . . not to mention the smell.

And what about the Gladiator boots. Remember them? They were the polished leather boots that hit just above the knee. You could look stylish in them or sit down. You couldn't do both.

The Diaper Bikini would have been a real seller if the wearers had been able to keep their weight down to eight-and-a-half pounds.

And the Fanny Sweater was a big loser. This was one of the many knit styles designed to fit a hanger and not the human body. The name was deceiving. It suggested that everyone who had a fanny should cover it with a sweater. In many instances, that's all the sweater covered and the sides and front were left wide open.

The Satin Pillow stomach just didn't make it. A few years ago, the manufacturer actually came out with a fake satin stomach that you tied around your waist for those girls who wanted to look healthy.

I looked so healthy in it, two men on the bus hoisted me into their seats and another called the police to report I was in the final stages of delivery. (The fake stomach now resides on the living room sofa.)

If there was ever a loser, however, it was the jumpsuit. This one-piece apparel has to be the Brand X of the fashion industry.

By actual count, there are only six women in the country who looked well in a jumpsuit. Five of them were terminal and the other was sired by a Xerox machine.

Just out of curiosity, I was rummaging

through a rack of jumpsuits when a saleswoman approached and asked, "Which size are you looking for? Twelve? Fourteen? Sixteen?"

"Yes," I said.

"Which?" she pursued.

"All three. My bust is twelve, my waist is a fourteen, and my hips are 16."

"Try the fourteen," she said dryly. "The fitting room is behind better dresses."

The fitting room was something I had never seen before. It was a community deal . . . a large room with sixteen mirrors on the wall, a rack in the center to hang discards and a woman by the door to make sure you didn't wear out anymore than you wore in.

Now a fitting room to me has always been like a confessional . . . where my body and my contrition take up the entire room. There is no room for anyone else. I looked around. All eyes seemed to be focused on one woman. She weighed about six pounds and was trying on a jumpsuit. It slid on easily, up over her hips and onto her arms. I winced as she distributed the cloth left over around her waist.

The crowd could not take their eyes off her. I had seen that look of resentment and pain on only one other occasion. It was a Charlton Heston movie just before the door slid back between the Christians and the Lions.

Inching closer, I whispered, "Lady, you better get out of here before they tear you to shreds."

It was my turn. For fifteen minutes, I tugged and inched my way into the jumpsuit and looked into the mirror. The chest was disguised as a back, the stomach strained at the buttons, the legs were numb without circulation and the hems swirled around the floor.

"How do you . . ."

"You swear off liquids after 4 P.M.," she said.

Or what about the platform shoes that brought about dizziness and nose bleeds? Also a broken leg to a thirteen-year-old girl in England, who fell off them.

Why the first time I tried on a pair of those Klutzies, I said to myself, "These shoes should have a label in them that reads, **"Warning: according to the Surgeon General's Office, these could be injurious to your health."**

I always thought platform shoes were something Alan Ladd wore to make kissing easier. Then I saw them on a woman who frequents my beauty shop. At first, I tried to ignore her deformity (Mother always said, "Don't stare. They know where their problem is located"). Finally, she said, "What do you think of my wedgies?"

"I know you can walk on water in them," I said, "But what else can you do?"

"Surely you jest," she said. "For a short person such as yourself, it could change your world. They can raise you off the ground, stretch out your body and make you look twenty pounds thinner. How tall are you? And how much do you weigh?"

I had no intention of giving her my vital statistics. "Let me put it this way," I said. "According to my girth, I should be a ninety-foot redwood."

"So, you need platforms," she said.

The first pair I tried on felt great. I wiggled my toes and they sprang back like a released arrow. My ankles felt firm and I felt tall.

Then I stood up.

Easing my way across the floor, I looked into a mirror. The reflection looked like Milton Berle with a migraine.

"How come you look so funny?" asked one of my children.

"Don't talk to me," I snapped. "I am busy keeping my shoes on."

In five minutes, I felt pain. In the back of my legs, running up my hips and finally down to my toes. Within an hour, my heels were purple and my toes felt like they were being pushed through a ballpoint pen.

The physical pain is nothing when you consider that the shoes cost eighteen dollars and that I don't throw a pair away until the soles are worn thin . . . and the soles are four-inches thick and by the time I get out of those orthopedic nightmares, I'll be a petrified redwood!

There is one fashion that never really comes in style and never seems to go out.

Each year, some designer comes out with the organized handbag. Now, I am not into organized handbags. Let me put it another way. If Monty Hall had offered a million dollars to anyone having a 1958 baby tooth, a set of keys to a three-year-old car, a fuzzy breath mint, and a half pair of footlets in their purse, I'd be a millionaire today.

As with most vices, the only people this bothers are the reformers. The people who want to make organized handbags into law. They're the do-gooders who won't rest until you put your car keys on a clip with a flashlight at the top of the bag in a spot marked "KEYS."

Actually, one of the more zealous members of the Organized Handbag Movement is my mother. She cannot comprehend why I carry around a pack of gum with no gum in it, or what possible use I will have for two "C" batteries. For my birthday, she couldn't wait to give me one of those handbags that has a place for everything. It looked like a Post Office.

"The first thing we're going to do is to sit down and get it all organized," she said, "and you'll never have to rummage through your purse again. Give me your checkbook."

"I don't have it," I said. "I just carry a few blank checks."

"What do you record them on when you have written them?"

"My grocery tape."

"Where do you keep the grocery tape?"

"In the brown bags where I get my groceries."

"And they are . . . ?"

"Under the sink waiting for the garbage."

"I see. Well now, where's your passport?"

"My what?"

"Your passport. You know, permission to enter a foreign country."

"I only use it when I enter your grandson's bedroom."

"And here's a bag for your makeup. Where is that?"

"I'm wearing it."

"Look," she said, "why don't you fill up all these little pockets and openings yourself and surprise me."

A few days later she saw the handbag and began to check it out. I had put all my raffle tickets under TRAVELER'S CHECKS, my hair clips and single earrings under CLUB AFFILIATIONS, the trading stamps jammed in the PASSPORT pocket, a pair of fake eyelashes under MAJOR CREDIT CARDS and two worn-out washers that I have to replace were in the MAKEUP bag.

As I told her, "I hope you're happy now. I won't be able to find a thing."

Another trend I cannot bear that is destined to race to oblivion is the name-dropping signatures that adorn everything you wear these days. I know a lot of women (two) who walk around looking like billboards. Their bags carry the Gucci signature, their scarves spell out Yves Saint-Laurent, and their blouses have the name of Wayne Rogers incorporated in the design.

I never know who makes my clothes. Whoever they are, they're too ashamed to sign 'em. The closest I ever came to finding out was when I shook a pair of slacks one day and a little piece of paper fell out: "INSPECTED BY 56." I have no idea who 56 is, or where she came from, but by wearing the slacks, I got a mental picture of Inspector 56. She was a former designer for an awning company until her vision started to go. When she could no longer see to attach a zipper to a tent flap, she was put in slacks. She regards slacks like a tent . . . one size fits all.

I tried to track her down, but I heard she changed her name to Inspector 94. Like I say, it doesn't bother me a bit that kids walk around in Hang Ten sweat sox with the two little feet emblem, or flaunt Levi labels coming out of their seams, but my friend is a real status seeker.

At lunch one day she gasped, "Did you see that! Violet is wearing a LANVIN blouse."

"How can you tell?"

"If you just read her chest, you can tell," she said.

"That's shabby. If people can't look at my clothes and by their style and cut know who designed them, I'm certainly not going to advertise."

"Don't give me that," she snapped. "If

your dresses had a perma-press label in them, you'd wear them wrong-side out."

That was a pretty rotten accusation from a woman I personally knew sat up nights drawing penguins on her husband's golf shirts. Like I told her, "You're such a snob it would serve you right if you got stuck with one of those fifty-dollar handbags that came out about a year ago. It seems a couple of designers subtly included an eight letter noun with an obscene word woven into the pattern. English-speaking women didn't have any idea that the word was smutty."

As my friend counted the letters out on her fingers, she exclaimed, "You don't have to tell me the word . . . just nod your head if I'm right. It's J. C. Penney, isn't it?"

"It is not J. C. Penney."

"You know the trouble with you," said my friend, "is that you're not open to new fashion trends. It takes a lot of courage to be different and you don't have the guts. Why, I bet you've never worn a bathrobe to a party, have you?"

"Not since the night I had my appendix

taken out on the coffee table.''

"Barbara Walters did," she said. "She was invited to a state dinner in the Philippines. The dinner was to begin in ten minutes and Barbara had not brought along a long dress. She was about to decline when she remembered she had a red bathrobe that would work, and saved the day. How does that make you feel?"

"Sick to my stomach."

I don't have a bathrobe in my drawer that would get me through an eighth-grade prom . . . or a house call from my doctor for that matter. Somehow, I cannot imagine myself showing up for a state dinner at the Philippines in a pair of blue scuffies, a flannel robe with a stomach button missing, spit-up on the shoulder (the baby is eighteen years old) and pockets bulging from nose tissue that smells like vapor-rub.

I even took a turn the other day through the lingerie department, and frankly I can see how they got away with it. I've never seen so many beautiful gowns and robes in my entire life.

"Here's one that's a luv," said the salesperson.

She held up a satin gown. (The last time I saw anything that narrow, there was toothpaste in it.)

"I'm afraid not. I have made it a rule of thumb that I do not wear anything to bed I have to wear a girdle under."

"What about this one?" she asked holding up a transparent bit of nylon.

"I have also promised myself that I would never wear anything in bed that you had to wear a coat over."

"What did you have in mind?" she asked.

"Something with sleeves, a turtleneck . . . and a zip-in floor."

Then she held up a robe. I have to tell you it was a knockout. "I'll take it," I said impishly.

Last weekend, I took the plunge and decided to wear it as an evening dress. Maybe my friend was right. As I entered the room . . . all eyes were upon me when my husband looked up and said, "Hurry up and get dressed. We're leaving in ten minutes."

There were other "losers" of course too numerous to mention. Who could forget the tube dress designed for the woman who wanted to be mailed somewhere, or the oriental look that lasted as long as our diplomatic relations with China lasted, or the pierced ears fad. I knew that would never last.

My daughter was crazy to have it done and I couldn't talk her out of it. I told her, "If the operation was so simple, Good Housekeeping would have put out a kit on it."

We both went to the department store jewelry counter where they had a chair for the puncturee.

"I'll watch," I said.

When I came to, my head was in Baked Goods and my feet in Better Sportswear.

"Is it over?" I gasped.

"Yes," said my daughter, "you did fine. You passed out just after you asked the anesthesiologist what kind of anesthetic he used and he turned out to be the jewelry buyer. See my earrings?"

She flipped back eight pounds of hair to reveal a little gold ring the size of a comma in her earlobe.

It was hardly worth my scrubbing up for.

11

How to Speak Child Fluently

One evening at the kitchen table, after the dishes had been cleared away, my son sat there writing feverishly in a spiral notebook.

"What are you doing?" I asked.

"An English assignment," he said. "On things my mother taught me."

I cast my eyes downward, trying to look humble. "Mind if I read it when you're finished?" He shook his head. An hour later, I settled down to what he had written.

Things My Mother Taught Me

LOGIC

If you fall off your bicycle and break your neck, you can't go to the store with me.

MEDICINE

If you don't stop crossing your eyes, they are going to freeze that way. There is no cure, no telethon, and no research program being funded at the moment for frozen eyes.

ESP

Put your sweater on. Don't you think *I* know when *YOU'RE* cold?

FINANCE

I told you the tooth fairy is writing checks because computerized billing is easier for the IRS.

CHALLENGE

Where is your sister and don't talk with food in your mouth. Will you answer me?!

HAPPINESS

You are going to have a good time on this vacation if we have to break every bone in your body.

HUMOR

When that lawn mower cuts off your toes, don't come running to me.

I will never understand children. I never pretended to. I meet mothers all the time who make resolutions to themselves. "I'm going to develop patience with my children and go out of my way to show them I am interested in them and what they do. I am going to understand my children." These women wind up making rag rugs, using blunt scissors.

I firmly believe kids don't want your

understanding. They want your trust, your compassion, your blinding love and your car keys, but you try to understand them and you're in big trouble. To me, they remain life's greatest mysteries.

I have never understood, for example, how come a child can climb up on the roof, scale the TV antenna and rescue the cat . . . yet cannot walk down the hallway without grabbing both walls with his grubby hands for balance.

Or how come a child can eat yellow snow, kiss the dog on the lips, chew gum that he found in the ashtray, put his mouth over a muddy garden hose . . . and refuse to drink from a glass his brother has just used.

Why is it he can stand with one foot on first base while reaching out and plucking a baseball off the ground with the tips of his fingers . . . yet cannot pick up a piece of soap before it melts into the drain.

I've seen kids ride bicycles, run, play ball, set up a camp, swing, fight a war, swim and race for eight hours, . . . yet have to be driven to the garbage can.

It puzzles me how a child can see a

dairy bar three miles away, but cannot see a 4 x 6 rug that has scrunched up under his feet and has been dragged through two rooms. Maybe you know why a child can reject a hot dog with mustard served on a soft bun at home, yet eat six of them two hours later at fifty cents each.

Did you ever wonder how you can trip over a kid's shoes under the kitchen sink, in the bathroom, on the front porch, under the coffee table, in the sandbox, in the car, in the clothes hamper and on the washer . . . but can never find them when it is time to cut grass?

If child raising were to be summed up in one word, it's frustration. You think you're on the inside track and you find you're still in the starting gate. It's not that you expect dividends on what you're doing . . . only a few meager returns.

Okay, take the car incident. My oldest took her car to the garage for repairs last week and used my car while hers was being fixed.

For three days I sat home without wheels (which is like telling Zsa Zsa

Gabor she can't have any more wedding cake).

On the day her car came back she returned my car keys and said, "Hey Mom, you owe me three dollars for the gas I put in your car".

I could not believe what she was saying. These words were being uttered by a child I poured eight hundred and eighty-seven dollars' worth of vitamins down. Paid one hundred fifty-four dollars for her old teeth under the pillow. Indulged in two thousand dollars' worth of toys (batteries extra). Foot the bill for one hundred eighty-six skin preparations to kill a single pimple. Sent to camp. Took the sink apart to find her lost class ring. Worried myself sick when she cracked an A in human sexuality.

Then I remembered a letter that a teenager had written me after she had read one of my books. Maybe that would get through to her.

"Listen to this," I said, reading from the letter.

"Parents go through life, Mrs.

Bombeck, saying to their children, 'I've worked my fingers to the bone for you. I've made sacrifices and what do I get in return?'

"You want an answer, Mrs. Bombeck? You get messy rooms, filthy clothing, disheveled hair, dirty fingernails, raided refrigerators ad nauseam. You get something else too. You get someone who loves you but never takes the time to tell you in words. You get someone who'll defend you at every turn even though you do wear orthopedic socks and enjoy listening to Pat Boone and changing your underwear everyday and acknowledging their presence in public.

"Yes, sometimes you talked too much and sometimes you turned away too soon. But you laughed with us and cried with us and all the agony, noncommunication, frustrations, fears and angers showed us that despite the need to be free and independent and do our own thing . . . you cared.

"And when we leave home, there will be a little tug at our hearts because we *know we will miss you and home and everything it meant. But most of all, we will miss the constantly assured knowledge of how very much you love us."*

My daughter looked up. Her eyes were misty. "Does that mean I don't get the three bucks?"

In a way, I blame experts for the mess parents are in today. They laid a ton of guilt on us so that we questioned every move we made.

I read one psychologist's theory that said, "Never strike a child in anger." When could I strike him? When he is kissing me on my birthday? When he is recuperating from measles? Do I slap the Bible out of his hand on a Sunday?

Another expert said, "Be careful in the way you discipline your children or you could permantly damage their Id."

Damage it! I didn't even know where it was. For all I knew it either made you sterile or caused dandruff. Once I suspected where it was, I made the kid wear four diapers just to be safe.

And scratch the wonderful "pal" theory that worked so great with our parents. My son slouched into the kitchen one night, threw his books on the countertop and said, "I've just had the worst day of my entire life and it's all your fault."

"How do you figure that?" I asked.

"Just because you made me go back up to my room and turn off all the lights before I went to school, I missed the bus. Then, with all your nagging about cleaning up my room, I couldn't find my gym clothes and got fifteen points knocked off my grade."

"The gym clothes were folded in your bottom drawer."

"Yeah, well, what yo-yo would expect them to be there?"

"You've got a point."

"I hope you're happy," he grumbled. "I have failed English."

"I did that?"

"That's right. I told you I had a paper that was due before lunch and you made me turn my lights off last night and wouldn't let me do it."

"It was one-thirty in the morning."

"Just forget it. It's done. Did you have a good lunch today? I hope so because, thanks to you, I didn't get any."

"What's THAT got to do with me?"

"You're the one who wouldn't advance me next week's allowance. And more good news. You know the suede jacket you got me for my birthday last year? Well, it's gone."

"And I'm to blame for that?"

"I'm glad you admit it. All I hear around here is, 'Hang up your coat, hang up your pajamas, hang up your sweater . . .' and the one time I take your advice and hang up my jacket on a hook in the lunchroom, someone rips it off. If I had just dropped it on the floor by my feet like I always do, I'd have that suede jacket today."

"It sounds like quite a day."

"It's not over yet," he said. "Didn't you forget something?"

"Like what?" I asked.

"Like, weren't you supposed to remind me I had ball practice after school?"

"I put a note on your desk."

"Under all that junk I'm supposed to

find a note! It would serve you right if I got cut. And I might just do that. I swear, I was talking to some of the guys and we decided parents can sure screw up their kids."

I smiled. "We try."

In analyzing the problem of parenting and understanding children, it would seem inevitable that this country will eventually resort to a Parental Park 'N' Swap.

I have never met a child who did not feel that he is maligned, harassed and overworked and would do better if he had Mrs. Jones for a mother who loves untidiness and eats out a lot.

On the other hand, I have never met a parent who did not feel unappreciated, persecuted, servile and would have been better off with Rodney Phipps who doesn't talk with food in his mouth and bought his mother a hair dryer for Mother's Day.

What I'm suggesting is a Sears parking lot that could be made available every Saturday afternoon, where parents and their offspring could come to look, compare and eventually swap if they felt they could do better.

When I mentioned this to my card club, they fairly quivered with excitement. "I have always wanted to 'trade up' to a child who picked towels up off the floor," said Peg.

"I have one like that," said Dorothy. "But she's a drain stuffer. If it doesn't fit down the drain she lifts out the trap and shoves it down."

"That doesn't sound so bad," said Evelyn. "I'd take a drain stuffer over a shower freak anyday. Empties a forty-gallon water tank three times a day."

"At least she's clean," said June. "I'll swap someone a long-hair who is an endangered species. Someday he's going to get lost behind that hair and never find his way out again."

"LOOK," said Peg, "I'm going to make you an offer you can't refuse. I'll offer my towel dropper for a boy who never learned how to use the telephone and I'll throw in a three weeks' supply of clean underwear."

"I'll do you one better," I said. "I'll swap or trade a quiet boy who is never late to dinner, gets up when he is called, sits up straight, has just finished two years with his orthodontist, is reasonable to operate and doesn't play his stereo too loud. No offer is too ridiculous."

The entire card table put down their cards and leaned forward. Finally June asked, "What's the catch?"

"No catch. He just knows two words . . . 'You know?' "

Everyone went home keeping what they had and feeling better about it.

When does parenting end?

It all depends on how you regard your children. Do you see them as an appliance that is under warranty to perform and when they start to cost money, get rid of them?

Are they like an endowment policy you invest in for eighteen or twenty years and then return dividends through your decining years?

Or are they like a finely gilded mirror that reflects the owner in every way and one day when you see a flaw in it, a distortion or one tiny idea that is different from your own, you cast it out and declare yourself a failure.

I said to my husband one night, "I see our children as kites. You spend a lifetime trying to get them off the ground. You run with them until you're both breathless . . . they crash . . . you add a longer tail . . . they hit the rooftop . . . you pluck them out of the spouting . . . you patch and comfort, adjust and teach. You watch them lifted by the wind and assure them that someday they'll fly . . . Finally, they're airborne, but they need more string and with each twist of the ball of twine, there is a sadness that goes with the joy because the kite becomes more distant and somehow you know it won't be long before this beautiful creature will snap the lifeline binding you together and soar as it was meant to soar — free and alone."

"That was beautiful," said my husband. "Are you finished?"

"I think so. Why?"

"Because one of your kites just crashed into the garage door with his car . . . another is landing here with three surfboards with friends on them and the third is hung up at college and needs more string to come home for the holidays."

12

"Travel Is So Broadening I Bought a Maternity Dress to Wear Home"

My husband and I are not your standard jet setters who whip over to Southern France every year to get away from the "little people."

But when our twenty-fifth wedding anniversary rolled around I said to him, "I want to go someplace where they haven't seen my two dresses."

"That narrows it down to Europe," he said.

Because it was a good day and all the parts of our bodies were working, we optimistically chose a package tour that would take us to fifteen countries in twenty-one days. It was obvious that I would need a wardrobe that was not only versatile, but could fit into a gym bag.

That's when I ran into an incredible phenomenon . . . the preplanned, no-fault, can't miss, color-coordinated, basic wardrobe.

"This," said the salesperson, "is the Weekender. It has four basic pieces that will take you from a super casual afternoon to a formal evening. And here is the Fortnighter. It's an eleven-piece coordinated collection designed to meet all the fashion requirements of a three-week holiday. This, of course, is the Around-the-World in Eighty Days and forty-four pounds. It's twenty-two pieces that combine to make one hundred fifty-five outfits."

"This little stack of clothes weighs forty-four pounds?" I asked.

"Of course not. The clothes only weigh eight pounds. There's a thirty-six-pound can of deodorant that comes with it."

"How does it work?" I asked.

"You just press the nozzle and . . ."

"Not the deodorant! The wardrobe!"

"Simple. Here is your basic pantsuit. Take off the blouse, add a vest and you're ready for polo. Take off the slacks, put on the shorts and you're dressed for bicycling. Zip the lining into the shorts, add the halter and it's a bathing suit. Take the straps off the halter and it's a bra. Add a short skirt and you're ready for tennis.

"Now, turn the blouse inside out and it's a bathrobe. Turn down the cuffs on the slacks, take the belt off the overblouse and you're in your jammies."

"It certainly is versatile," I stammered.

"Versatile! Look at the accessories. This elasticized halter can get you a sun tan, but when pulled down over the hips is a girdle. Now slip into the evening skirt, slip on this veil and you're ready to be married. Or slap a monogram on the jacket and you can pass for a member of the U.S. Olympic Chess team. The long skirt is plastic-lined. If you have to, you could convert it into a tent and live out of it for a week. Or snap out the sleeves in the overblouse and it's a caftan.

"Take off the scarf, roll down the sleeves of the blouse, put it on backward, take off your underwear and it's a hospital gown. Trust me, there are enough combinations to mix and match for eighty days."

I was ready for our adventure.

When people talk about these package tours, they are always impressed by the fact that they are a bargain. You do so much and see so much, yet they are able to offer it at prices far below domestic travels at home. In analyzing this phenomenon one morning, we both concluded one of the reasons has to be the Continental Breakfast.

The Continental Breakfast consists of a paper napkin, a knife, fork and spoon for which you have no use, a cup and saucer, a pot of coffee or tea and a container of marmalade dated, "PLEASE USE

BEFORE JULY, 1936." Finally, two four-letter words that have come to strike terror in the hearts of travelers everywhere . . . the HARD ROLL.

The Continental Breakfast (literal translation: Keep out of the reach of children) has a gradual but unmistakable effect on people who eat it for a period of ten days or more.

For the first several days, partakers of the hard roll will pretend it is just the thing they need or the Famine Is Fun number. Women will pinch their waists and say, "I've been eating too much on this trip. A light breakfast is just what I need."

The truth is, the hard roll is not designed to take off weight. Even though eaten in small pieces, once in the body, it will form again in its original hard ball and build a solid wall across the hips and stomach. After the eleventh day, hard rolls make you mean.

We had our first hard roll in Italy on July first. By July fifteenth, the group was irritable and noncommunicative. On the seventeenth, while in Belgium, my husband, in a fit of violence, grabbed a hard roll, carved his initials in it, "WLB, 1977," and sent it back to the kitchen.

By the nineteenth day, the prospect of a hard roll for breakfast forced some travelers to remain in their beds with their faces turned to the wall. Others used the hard roll to pry open their luggage, prop open their doors, or to rub stubborn stains from their shirt collars.

I seemed to be surviving the Hard Roll trauma, but I was fighting Montezuma II's revenge. (Few people realize this, but there were two Montezumas. Montezuma I is credited with lending his name to an urgency Americans refer to as the Green Apple Two-step. Montezuma II is generally known as the patron saint of gift shops. Both are unkind to foreigners.)

With Montezuma II's revenge, I would be in the country no longer than five minutes before I got severe stomach cramps, my right hand would stiffen into the shape of a credit card holder, my step would quicken and I'd rush out into the streets shouting, "How much? How much?"

Sometimes, early in the morning, I'd leave my room and wander through the hotel lobby mumbling, "I smell gift shops. I couldn't sleep."

Somehow, I was like a woman obsessed. I bought a head scarf that when worn in the rain gave me a navy blue face. I bought a toilet tissue holder carved out of wood and held by a man with one tooth. I bought keyrings, flags, bongo drums, patches, and a left-handed letter opener made out of reindeer antlers.

After a while, I couldn't sit on a sightseeing bus for longer than an hour or so before leaning over to the bus driver and saying, "Aren't we going to make a gift-shop stop soon?"

"Is it absolutely necessary?" he'd plead.

"Are you willing to take a chance it isn't?"

I bought boxes of matches, T-shirts, paperweights, pennants, and ships in bottles, small glass ducks, corkscrews, and rocks with the Lord's Prayer on them.

I bought a moose for my charm

bracelet, a cocktail apron, three cheese slicers with fur handles, a Spanish doll for my bed, a small chicken coming out of a soapstone egg, ashtrays, a set of coasters, a linen calendar with months I couldn't translate, and a wild boar cookbook.

By the twenty-first day, we could barely board the plane.

Besides, I was carrying a papier-mâché donkey with a wire holder that was severing my ring finger.

I jammed a shopping bag of souvenirs under the seat in front of me.

"You're supposed to fold your snack tray up before we take off," said my husband.

"This is not a snack tray. It's my stomach."

The stewardess came by later with lunch. My husband picked up the hard roll and ran his fingers over it. There was WLB-1977 carved on the side.

We both agreed it was probably a coincidence.

13

The Trick Is Knowing When to Laugh . . .

A lot of people think I write humor.

But then I know a woman who thinks Marie Osmond and her relatives are depressed. As an observer of the human condition all I do is question it. I rarely find it funny.

For example, how come pens never have any ink in them except when they get in the washer by mistake and the entire laundry turns blue?

Why do they waste silicone on an ironing board cover?

How can an owner of a vicious dog look at his dog baring his teeth and know he is "smiling?"

Why is there a rectal thermometer in my sewing basket?

Why do I assume those two doves nuzzling in the trees are married? Maybe they're just fooling around.

How come the first thing I notice in a doctor's office is whether or not his plants are dead?

Okay, so maybe my threshold of laughter is. low, but if you can find anything funny in the following items, I'll make a book out of 'em.

Microphones

If there is anything in this world as fiercely independent as a microphone, I don't know what it is.

I mean, imagine the year is 1775. At the Provincial Convention in Virginia, statesman Patrick Henry rises to his feet to make an impassioned plea for liberty or death. He approaches the microphone and as the entire assembly awaits his first words he asks, "Can everyone in the back hear me?"

Those seven words have preceded more speeches than the proverbial cocktail hour.

In ten years of lecturing, I have seen microphones go from an occasional passive screech to real screaming militancy. To begin with, microphones do not like to be touched by a union or otherwise. Because I am short, I tried to adjust one the other week. I gave it just a simple tweak, mind you, and it went as limp as a two-dollar permanent in a sauna. I gave the entire speech from a squatting sprinter's position.

Some microphones work great as long as you blow into them. So you stand there like an idiot blowing and saying, "Are we on? Can you hear me?" Everyone admits they can hear you blowing. It's only when you speak the microphone goes dead.

Others have a weird sense of humor. They're punchline poopers. You'll be sailing along with a three-minute story, building to a big pitch and just as you say, "So why isn't the dog drinking his

187

daiquiri?'' the microphone goes silent and you're left muttering, ''Gee, I guess you had to have been there.''

Some speakers spend half their lives looking for the on / off switch of microphones. There aren't any. I've looked for them under the light, on the shelf, on the side, the gooseneck, offstage. I suspect most of them are triggered by a remote control in a 1936 pickup truck in a garage across from the auditorium.

I have been warned that microphones are supersensitive and you have to talk right into them to be heard. These are usually the ones that cross you up by picking up your entire luncheon conversation including, ''My God, do you mean the management is charging you ten dollars for this lunch! Has he never heard of the Geneva Convention?''

Some speakers, more secure than I, have dared to make fun of microphones. Recently, book columnist and reviewer Bob Cromie spoke in our town and opened with the traditional, ''Can everyone in the back hear me?''

When someone yelled, ''no'' he said,

"Then how did you know what I asked?"

All night long that microphone floated toward the door. Didn't surprise me a bit.

No One Wins

Did you ever notice how in reporting sports no one ever "wins" a game?

They crush, stomp, triumph, trounce, bomb, outscore, outclass, overthrow, run over, edge out, hammer and victimize, but they never use the word "win."

The other night after a sportscast where there were three assaults, four upsets, one humiliation, a squeaker, and a rout, I said to my husband, "These guys must be fed intravenously by a thesaurus each night to come up with all those words that mean 'win.' "

"They have to," he said. "You'd get bored hearing who 'won' all the time."

"But that's not the way people talk," I complained. "Can't you just see some two-hundred-thirty-pound guard being interviewed at halftime saying, 'We came to best Pittsburgh. At this moment, we're not overwhelming by as much as we had hoped, but sooner or later we hope to vanquish. After all, as Vince Lombardi said, 'subduing is everything.' ''

"You should talk," he said. "How come a woman on the society pages never 'gets married?' ''

"What are you talking about?"

"I've read those stories before. They 'exchange vows,' 'say nuptials' or 'pledge I do's,' but they never 'get married!' ''

"That's different."

"Why different? We're talking about saying what we mean. When we got engaged I suppose you called up your best friend and said, 'Hey, Dottie, guess what. I'm going to plight my troth in August.' ''

"I think plighting a troth is rather poetic. It's certainly not like the Raiders 'smothering' their opponents or the Jets 'clobbering' theirs."

"Hey," he grinned, "it might be fun if society pages showed as much imagination as they do on the sports pages. Can't you just imagine reading where 'Betty Schmidlapp cruised by four ugly bridesmaids Saturday to overpower her opponents and cap a victory in the Bridegroom Open in the upset of the year'?''

"This is a stupid argument," I said. "And I don't want to continue it. Just say I won and we'll forget it."

He sat there thinking.

"See," I continued. "You haven't heard the word win in so long you can't even remember how it goes."

"Let's see," he said, "let's just say in the sports vernacular you 'persuaded your opponent it was in his best interest to lose.' ''

The Unmailed Letter

I found a letter to my sister the other day that I had forgotten to mail.

It just needed a little updating to send. After "The baby is . . ." I crossed out "toilet trained" and wrote in "graduating from high school this month."

And in the P.S. where I had written "I found my first gray hair today," I ran a line through gray and substituted "black."

The rest of the letter was still current.

191

"I am on a diet as my skin does not fit me anymore. The children are rotten and I am slipping away from reality. I am going to paint the bathroom and write to the rest of the family next week."

The trouble with me is I don't like to write letters unless I have something exciting to report. I am intimidated by letter-writers whose correspondence electrifies you.

I have one group of friends who only write me once a year — from a cruise ship. They know it's going to make me spit up with jealousy and they write cute little messages that begin, "Luv: Thinking of you as we island-hop," and end with: "Must dash. A Robert Redford look-alike has been chasing me all over the ship."

Other pen-pals I can live without are the people whose children are overachievers. Their letters are filled with news of "Robbie" who just won a "Being" scholarship to Harvard. (He's so exceptional, all he has to do is sit there and breathe for four years.) There's also nine-year-old Rachel, who is competing in the Baton Olympics, makes all her own clothes, just sold her first story to *Reader's Digest,* and is going to spend her entire summer reading the Bible. And don't forget little Kenneth, who gets up during the night to change his own Pampers. (Does you-know-who still have a plastic liner in his football uniform?)

The letter-writers who really bug me, though, are the ones with the stationery whose paper matches the envelopes. Sure it's easy to write a letter when you have all the equipment, but for me, it's a real hassle finding clean paper, a pencil and a stamp.

I found a letter from my sister in the mailbox today. She had crossed out "I'm glad the war is over," and substituted "Christmas." She said they loved their new Edsel, which she ran a line through and added Datsun, and added she was going to clean her oven as we were approaching a month with R in it.

My sister and I are related through recessive Writer's Cramps.

Killing Your Mother

My son never fails to amaze me. At age twenty-one, he has come up with a new way to break his neck. It's called a skateboard.

Frankly, I'm tired. I've dedicated my entire life to keeping that kid whole and at a time of my life when I should be eating chocolate sandwiches and getting up at the crack of noon . . . I'm a a bundle of nerves.

It started with the two-wheel bicycle. As I ran along beside him, clutching his sweater with one hand and the bicycle seat with the other, I yelled, "You could kill yourself on this thing." Sure enough, my housecoat caught in the spokes and I almost made a wheel out of myself.

The Pogo stick was worse. As he sprung about the house, his head inches from the ceiling, I tried to shield him from falling into a lamp and he lost his balance . . . pinning me between the floor and his body, causing me severe pain.

When he wanted a horse, I tried to warn him that I just wasn't up to it, but did he listen? He did not. As I led the beast around by the reins, I was repaid for my vigilance by being stomped on by a fifteen-hundred pound horse.

"We are not going out for football," I told him the summer of his fifteenth year. "What do you mean what has that got to do with me? I'm your mother. If you want to kill your *mother,* I can't stop you, but every Mother's Day . . . mark my words . . . you're going to feel just terrible." (I carry with me today a trick knee suffered when I ran onto the playing field with an extra mouthpiece to protect fifteen-hundred dollars' worth of braces.)

It never ended. He jumped off the high board at the pool just to give me stomach cramps and as soon as I thought I had myself under control, he came home with his learner's permit to drive. (The only boy I know who was given a ticket for speeding . . . in reverse.)

I thought all of it was behind me until the other night when he was leaving the house with this little board with the wheels under his arm.

"Where are you going?" I asked.

"Trying to find an empty swimming pool, a hill, or a paved ditch. Then I am going to balance myself on this little board up the side of it until I fall off."

I climbed on the skateboard, clutched him around the waist and closed my eyes. "Why don't you like your mother?" I whimpered.

14

I'm Laughing So Hard I Can't Stop Crying

An interviewer once asked what the Bombeck family was "really" like. Did we seem as we are in print? A composite of the Bradys, Waltons, Osmonds and Partridges sitting around cracking one-liners.

The last time my family laughed was when my oven caught fire and we had to eat out for a week.

I did not get these varicose veins of the neck from whispering. We shout at one another. We say hateful things. We cry, slam doors, goof off, make mistakes, experience disappointments, tragedies, sickness and traumas. When I last checked, we were members in good standing of your basic screw-up family.

There is a thin line that separates laughter and pain, comedy and tragedy, humor and hurt.

And how do you know laughter if there is no pain to compare it with.

When Did I Become the Mother and the Mother Become the Child?

A nuclear physicist once figured out if a woman has a baby when she is twenty years old, she is twenty times as old as the baby.

When the baby is twenty years of age and the mother is forty, she is only twice as old as the child. When the baby is sixty and the mother is eighty, she is only 1 1/3 times as old as the child. When the child is eighty and the mother is one hundred, she is only 1¼ times as old as the offspring.

When will the baby catch up with the mother?

When indeed.

Does it begin one night when you are asleep and your mother is having a restless night and you go into her room and tuck the blanket around her bare arms?

Does it appear one afternoon when, in a moment of irritation, you snap, "How can I give you a home permanent if you won't sit still? If you don't care how you look, I do!" (My God, is that an echo?)

Or did it come the rainy afternoon when you were driving home from the store and you slammed on your brakes and your arms sprang protectively between her and the windshield and your eyes met with a knowing, sad look?

The transition comes slowly, as it began between her and her mother. The changing of power. The transferring of responsibility. The passing down of duty. Suddenly you are spewing out the familiar phrases learned at the knee of your mother.

"Of course you're sick. Don't you think I know when you're not feeling well? I'll be over to pick you up and take you to the doctor around eleven. And be ready!"

"So, where's your sweater? You know how cold the stores get with the air conditioning. That's the last thing you need is a cold."

"You look very nice today. Didn't I tell you you'd like that dress? The other one made you look too old. No sense looking old before you have to."

"Do you have to go to the bathroom before we go? You know what a big deal it is at the doctor's. You have to ask for the key and walk ten miles down all those corridors. Why don't you just go anyway . . . just to get it over with."

"If you're not too tired we'll shop. Did you take your nap this morning? When you get tired tell me and I'll take you home. You know I can't shop when you stand on one foot and then the other." (Good Lord, did you really tuck her arm in yours nearly pulling her feet off the floor?)

Rebellion? "I'll thank you, missy; to let me make my own decisions. I know when I'm tired, and when I am I have the good sense to go to bed. Stop treating me like a child!" She is not ready to step down yet.

But slowly and insidiously and certainly the years give way and there is no one to turn to.

"Where are my glasses? I never can find them. Did I fall asleep in the movie again? What was it all about?"

"Dial that number for me. You know how I always get the wrong one."

"I'm not having a Christmas tree this year. There's no one to see it and it just dirties up the carpet for eight months or so."

"Look what I made in macrame today. I'll make you a sling in blue for your kitchen if you want." (It is reminiscent of the small hand in plaster of paris framed over the sofa.)

"Where's my flight number and the times of my planes? You always type it out for me and put it in the airline ticket pocket. I can't read those little numbers."

Rebellion: "Mother really, you're not

that old. You can do things for yourself. Surely you can still see to thread your own needle.

"And you certainly aren't too tired to call up Florence and say hello. She's called you fifteen times and you never call her back. Why don't you have lunch with her sometimes. It would do you good to get out of the house."

"What do you mean you're overdrawn? Can't you remember to record your checks each time you write them?"

The daughter isn't ready yet to carry the burden. But the course is set.

The first year you celebrate Thanksgiving at your house and you roast the turkey and your mother sets the table.

The first time you subconsciously turn to her in a movie and say, "Shhhh!"

The first time you rush to grab her arm when she walks over a patch of ice.

As your own children grow strong and independent, the mother becomes more childlike.

"Mother, I did not take your *TV Guide* off the TV set."

"Did so."

"Did not."

"Did so."

"Did not."

"Did."

"Not."

"I saw your father last night and he said he would be late."

"You didn't see Dad last night. He's dead, Mother."

"Why would you say a thing like that? You're a terrible child."

("I saw Mr. Ripple and he swung me on the swings for hours."

"There is no Mr. Ripple. You made him up. He doesn't exist."

"That's not true. Why would you say that? Just because you don't see him doesn't mean he isn't there.")

"You never want to visit with me. You fiddle with those children too much. They don't even need you."

("Are you going to play bridge again? You always go out and you never have anytime to read me stories!")

"For goodness sake, Mom, don't mention Fred's hairpiece. We all know he has one and having you mention it doesn't help."

("You mind your manners, little girl, and don't speak unless you're spoken to.")

The daughter contemplates, "It wasn't supposed to be this way. All the years I was bathed, dressed, fed, advised, disciplined, ordered, cared for and had every need anticipated, I wanted my turn to come when I could command. Now that it's here, why am I so sad?"

You bathe and pat dry the body that once housed you. You spoon feed the lips that kissed your cuts and bruises and made them well. You comb the hair that used to playfully cascade over you to make you laugh. You arrange the covers over the legs that once carried you high into the air to Banbury Cross.

The naps are frequent as yours used to be. You accompany her to the bathroom and wait to return her to bed. She has a sitter already for New Year's Eve. You never thought it would be like this.

While riding with your daughter one day, she slams on her brakes and her arm flies out instinctively in front of you between the windshield and your body.

My God! So soon.

Mike and the Grass

When Mike was three he wanted a
sandbox and his father said, "There goes
the yard. We'll have kids over here day
and night and they'll throw sand into the
flower beds and cats will make a mess in
it and it'll kill the grass for sure."

And Mike's mother said, "It'll come
back."

When Mike was five, he wanted a jungle
gym set with swings that would take his
breath away and bars to take him to the
summit and his father said, "Good grief.
I've seen those things in backyards and do
you know what they look like? Mud holes
in a pasture. Kids digging their gum shoes
in the ground. It'll kill the grass.

And Mike's mother said, "It'll come
back."

Between breaths when Daddy was
blowing up the plastic swimming pool he
warned, "You know what they're going to
do to this place? They're going to

condemn it and use it for a missile site. I hope you know what you're doing. They'll track water everywhere and you'll have a million water fights and you won't be able to take out the garbage without stepping in mud up to your neck and when we take this down we'll have the only brown lawn on the block."

"It'll come back," smiled Mike's mother.

When Mike was twelve, he volunteered his yard for a campout. As they hoisted the tents and drove in the spikes his father stood at the window and observed, "Why don't I just put the grass seed out in cereal bowls for the birds and save myself the trouble of spreading it around? You know for a fact that those tents and all those big feet are going to trample down every single blade of grass, don't you? Don't bother to answer," he said. "I know what you're going to say, 'It'll come back.'"

The basketball hoop on the side of the garage attracted more crowds than the Winter Olympics. And a small patch of lawn that started out with a barren spot the size of a garbage can lid soon grew to encompass the entire side yard. Just when it looked like the new seed might take root, the winter came and the sled runners beat it into ridges and Mike's father shook his head and said, "I never asked for much in this life . . . only a patch of grass."

And his wife smiled and said, "It'll come back."

The lawn this fall was beautiful. It was green and alive and rolled out like a sponge carpet along the drive where gym shoes had trod . . . along the garage where bicycles used to fall . . . and around the flower beds where little boys used to dig with iced teaspoons.

But Mike's father never saw it. He anxiously looked beyond the yard and asked with a catch in his voice, "He will come back, won't he?"

My Turn

For years, you've watched everyone else do it.

The children who sat on the curb eating

their lunches while waiting for the bus.

The husband you put through school who drank coffee standing up and who slept with his hand on the alarm.

And you envied them and said, "Maybe next year I'll go back to school." And the years went by and this morning you looked into the mirror and said, "You blew it. You're too old to pick it up and start a new career."

This column is for you.

Margaret Mitchell won her first Pulitzer Prize for *Gone With the Wind* in 1937. She was thirty-seven years old at the time.

Sen. Margaret Chase Smith was elected to the Senate for the first time in 1948 at the age of fifty-one.

Ruth Gordon picked up her first Oscar in 1968 for *Rosemary's Baby*. She was seventy-two years old.

Billie Jean King took the battle of women's worth to a tennis court in Houston's Astrodome to outplay Bobby Riggs. She was thirty-one years of age.

Grandma Moses began a painting career at the age of seventy-six.

Anne Morrow Lindbergh followed in the shadow of her husband until she began to question the meaning of her own existence. She published her thoughts in *A Gift from the Sea* in 1955, in her forty-ninth year.

Shirley Temple Black was named Ambassador to Ghana at the age of forty-seven.

Golda Meir in 1969, was elected Prime Minister of Israel. She had just passed her seventy-first birthday.

You can tell yourself these people started out as exceptional. You can tell yourself they had influence before they started. You can tell yourself the conditions under which they achieved were different from yours.

Or you can be like the woman I knew who sat at her kitchen window year after year and watched everyone else do it. Then one day she said, "I do not feel fulfilled cleaning chrome faucets with a toothbrush. It's my turn."

I was thirty-seven years old at the time.

Beauty

According to her height and weight on the insurance charts, she should be a guard for the Lakers.

She has iron-starved blood, one shoulder is lower than the other, and she bites her fingernails.

She is the most beautiful woman I have ever seen. She should be. She's worked on that body and face for more than sixty years. The process for that kind of beauty can't be rushed.

The wrinkles in the face have been earned . . . one at a time. The stubborn one around the lips that deepened with every ''No.'' The thin ones on the forehead that mysteriously appeared when the first child was born.

The eyes are protected by glass now, but you can still see the perma-crinkles around them. Young eyes are darting and fleeting. These are mature eyes that reflect a lifetime. Eyes that have glistened with pride, filled with tears of sorrow, snapped in anger, and burned from loss of sleep. They are now direct and penetrating and look at you when you speak.

The bulges are classics. They developed slowly from babies too sleepy to walk who had to be carried home from Grandma's, grocery bags lugged from the car, ashes carried out of the basement while her husband was at war. Now, they are fed by a minimum of activity, a full refrigerator and TV bends.

The extra chin is custom-grown and takes years to perfect. Sometimes you can only see it from the side but it's there. Pampered women don't have an extra chin. They cream them away or pat the muscles until they become firm. But this chin has always been there, supporting a nodding head that has slept in a chair all night . . . bent over knitting . . . praying.

The legs are still shapely, but the step is slower. They ran too often for the bus, stood a little too long when she "clerked" in the department store, got beat up while teaching her daughter how to ride a two-wheeler. They're purple at the back of the knees.

The hands? They're small and veined

and have been dunked, dipped, shook, patted, wrung, caught in doors, splintered, dyed, bitten and blistered, but you can't help but be impressed when you see the ring finger that has shrunk from years of wearing the same wedding ring. It takes time — and much more — to diminish a finger.

I looked at Mother long and hard the other day and said, "Mom, I have never seen you so beautiful." "I work at it," she snapped.

"You Don't Love Me"

"You don't love me!"

How many times have your kids laid that one on you?

And how many times have you, as a parent, resisted the urge to tell them how much?

Someday, when my children are old enough to understand the logic that motivates a mother, I'll tell them.

I loved you enough to bug you about where you were going, with whom, and what time you would get home.

I loved you enough to insist you buy a bike with your own money that we could afford and you couldn't.

I loved you enough to be silent and let you discover your hand-picked friend was a creep.

I loved you enough to make you return a Milky Way with a bite out of it to a drugstore and confess, "I stole this."

I loved you enough to stand over you for two hours while you cleaned your bedroom, a job that would have taken me fifteen minutes.

I loved you enough to say, "Yes, you can go to Disney World on Mother's Day."

I loved you enough to let you see anger, disappointment, disgust and tears in my eyes.

I loved you enough not to make excuses for your lack of respect or your bad manners.

I loved you enough to admit that I was wrong and ask your forgiveness.

I loved you enough to ignore "what every other mother" did or said.

I loved you enough to let you stumble, fall, hurt and fail.

I loved you enough to let you assume the responsibility for your own actions, at six, ten, or sixteen.

I loved you enough to figure you would lie about the party being chaperoned, but forgave you for it . . . after discovering I was right.

I loved you enough to shove you off my lap, let go of your hand, be mute to your pleas . . . so that you had to stand alone.

I loved you enough to accept you for what you are, not what I wanted you to be.

But most of all, I loved you enough to say no when you hated me for it. That was the hardest part of all.

Are You Listening?

It was one of those days when I wanted my own apartment . . . unlisted.

My son was telling me in complete detail about a movie he had just seen, punctuated by three thousand "You know's?" My teeth were falling asleep.

There were three phone calls — strike that — three monologues that could have been answered by a recording. I fought the urge to say, "It's been nice listening to you."

In the cab from home to the airport, I got another assault on my ear, this time by a cab driver who was rambling on about his son whom he supported in college, and was in his last year, who put a P.S. on his letter saying, "I got married. Her name is Diane." He asked me, "What do you think of that?" and proceeded to answer the question himself.

There were thirty whole beautiful minutes before my plane took off . . . time for me to be alone with my own thoughts, to open a book and let my mind wander. A voice next to me belonging to an elderly woman said, "I'll bet it's cold in Chicago."

Stone-faced, I answered, "It's likely."

"I haven't been to Chicago in nearly three years," she persisted. "My son lives there."

"That's nice," I said, my eyes intent on the printed page of the book.

"My husband's body is on this plane. We've been married for fifty-three years. I don't drive, you know, and when he died a nun drove me from the hospital. We aren't even Catholic. The funeral director let me come to the airport with him.''

I don't think I have ever detested myself more than I did at that moment. Another human being was screaming to be heard and in desperation had turned to a cold stranger who was more interested in a novel than the real-life drama at her elbow.

All she needed was a listener . . . no advice, wisdom, experience, money, assistance, expertise or even compassion . . . but just a minute or two to listen.

It seemed rather incongruous that in a society of supersophisticated communication, we often suffer from a shortage of listeners.

She talked numbly and steadily until we boarded the plane, then found her seat in another section. As I hung up my coat, I heard her plaintive voice say to her seat companion, ''I'll bet it's cold in Chicago.''

I prayed, ''Please God, let her listen.''

Why am I telling you this? To make me feel better. It won't help, though.

The Chimes

Everything is in readiness.

The tree is trimmed. The cards taped to the doorframe. The boxes stacked in glittering disarray under the tree.

Why don't I hear chimes?

Remember the small boy who made the chimes ring in a fictional story years ago? As the legend went, the chimes would not ring unless a gift of love was placed on the altar. Kings and men of great wealth placed untold jewels on the altar, but year after year the church remained silent.

Then one Christmas Eve, a small child in a tattered coat made his way down the aisle and without anyone noticing he took off his coat and placed it on the altar. The chimes rang out joyously throughout the land to mark the unselfish giving of a small boy.

I used to hear chimes.

I heard them the year one of my sons gave me a tattered piece of construction paper on which he had crayoned two hands folded in prayer and a moving message, "OH COME HOLY SPIT!"

217

I heard them the year I got a shoebox that contained two baseball cards and the gum was still with them.

I heard them the Christmas they all got together and cleaned the garage.

They're gone, aren't they? The years of the lace doilies fashioned into snowflakes . . . the hands traced in plaster of paris . . . the Christmas trees of pipe cleaners . . . the thread spools that held small candles. They're gone.

The chubby hands that clumsily used up two dollars' worth of paper to wrap a cork coaster are sophisticated enough to take a number and have the gift wrapped professionally.

The childish decision of when to break the ceramic piggybank with a hammer to spring the fifty-nine cents is now resolved by a credit card.

The muted thump of pajama-covered feet padding down the stairs to tuck her homemade crumb scrapers beneath the tree has given way to pantyhose and fashion boots to the knee.

It'll be a good Christmas. We'll eat too much. Make a mess in the living room.

Throw the warranties into the fire by mistake. Drive the dog crazy taping bows to his tail. Return cookies to the plate with a bite out of them. Listen to Christmas music.

But Lord . . . what I would give to bend low and receive a gift of toothpicks and library paste and hear the chimes just one more time.

Epilogue

When you're an othodox worrier, some days are worse than others.

I pride myself on being able to handle traumas, natural disasters, deep depression, misfortune, hardship, discomfort, and readily adjust when they run out of extra crispy chicken at the carry-out.

But last week, you would not believe that even a professional pessimist could have survived what I went through.

It began on Monday when the kids filed into the kitchen completely dressed.

I stood there with my iron (the one with the fifty-foot cord) and asked, "Who wants something pressed before you go to school?'' No one moved!

My car with the new battery actually started. I found a parking place in front of the supermarket, got a shopping cart with four wheels that all went in the same direction at the same time, and found a sale on something edible that I needed. That night, on television, Angie Dickinson looked a little fat. I cooked a dinner that no one had had for lunch.

All of that began to make me feel a little edgy, but I figured by the next day things would surely get back to normal. They didn't. At the library, all four of the books I had written were checked out. I took a bath and the phone didn't ring. I sewed up a skirt and with two inches left to do, the bobbin didn't even run out of thread. I went to bed thinking things had to get worse tomorrow . . . they couldn't get any better.

On Wednesday, I ran for a bus and made it. The dentist said I had no cavities. The phone was ringing when I arrived home and even after I dropped my key a couple of times, I answered it and they were still on the line. The Avon lady refused me service saying I didn't need her as I already looked terrific. My husband asked me what kind of a day I had and didn't leave the room when I started to answer.

By Thursday, I was a basket case anticipating what was in store for me, but it didn't happen. My daughter told me my white socks looked good with wedgies. The checkbook balanced. No one snacked and ruined their dinners, and a film at the school, *The History of Sulphur,* was canceled.

On Friday, I was sobbing into a dishtowel when my husband tried to comfort me, "I can't help it," I said, "things were never meant to go this well. I'm worried."

"Now, now," he said patting my shoulder, "things can't go rotten all the time. How could we appreciate the bad times if we don't have a good day once in a while."

"I know I'm going to get it," I said. "Do you know that yesterday I went into the boys' room and their beds were made? (He frowned.) And that we got a note from the IRS apologizing for being late with our refund? This isn't like us," I whined. "The bad times I can handle. It's the good times that drive me crazy. When is the other shoe going to drop?"

We heard a car turn into the garage and make the sickening scrape of a fender when it meets an immovable wall.

We looked at each other and smiled. Things are looking up.

The publishers hope that this Large Print Book has brought you pleasurable reading. Each title is designed to make the text as easy to see as possible. G. K. Hall Large Print Books are available from your library or local bookstore or through the Large Print Book Club. If you would like a complete list of the Large Print Books we have published or information about our Book Club, please write directly to:

G. K. Hall & Co.
70 Lincoln Street
Boston, Mass. 02111